C++: The Core Language

C++: The Core Language

Gregory Satir and Doug Brown

O'Reilly & Associates, Inc.

Cambridge · *Köln* · *Paris* · *Sebastopol* · *Tokyo*

C++: The Core Language
by Gregory Satir and Doug Brown

Copyright © 1995 O'Reilly & Associates, Inc. All rights reserved.
Printed in the United States of America.

Editor: Adrian Nye

Production Editor: Mary Anne Weeks Mayo

Printing History:

October 1995:	First Edition.
August 1996:	Minor corrections.

This book is printed on acid-free paper with 85% recycled content, 15% post-consumer waste. O'Reilly & Associates is committed to using paper with the highest recycled content available consistent with high quality.

ISBN: 1-56592-116-X   [5/97]

Table of Contents

Preface

This book is for C programmers who want to learn C++. Why assume C and why write about C++? We assume you're a C programmer because you need to learn most of C to learn C++. We see no reason to write yet another C primer when so many good ones already exist. But we *don't* think there are plenty of good C++ books already. Not for beginners, anyway. We explain what we think is inadequate with the existing books, and what is better with this one, in the two sections following the next. First we'll say a little about what C++ is.

What Is C++?

C++ is essentially C with extensions for object-oriented programming (OOP). One might argue that some of the extensions aren't really for OOP, but the majority of them clearly are. C++ is mostly a superset of C, but there are a few things that C++ changed. We describe the changes in Chapter 2, *C++ Without Classes.*

An important feature of C++ is that it is still changing. At this time there is no C++ standard. There are ANSI and ISO committees working on writing one, but for now the closest you can get to a standard is the latest ANSI/ISO proposed standard, which continues to change. That hasn't stopped several major software vendors from selling C++ compilers and millions of programmers from using them. Compiler vendors are simply implementing features as they make it into the proposed standard.

Does this continual state of flux mean that the committees could make some huge change and invalidate all your code? No way. There are probably billions of lines of commercially developed C++ code in use throughout the world. That means there are two things stopping the standardization effort from veering wildly off course. One is that the members of the committees deciding on the standard have a vested interest in a large portion of those lines of code. Another is that, even if the standard suddenly changed, existing programs need to be maintained. So, there's a market for compiler vendors to continue to support those programs, whether the language is called C++ or whatever.

What the fluctuating standard does mean is that you need to do two things. One is be careful about what features you use if you want your code to be portable. You should be shy about using the latest features of the proposed standard until all the major compiler vendors have implemented them. Another is to be prepared to grow with the language. Excellent C++ programs written in 1989 might not look so good today. There are now better ways to handle some sticky problems that had no easy solutions in 1989.

There will be fewer major additions to the language itself in the future, but there will still be significant changes around it. The standardization of a C++ library is one possibility. A growing body of shared C++ experience is another. The latter is far more important than you might guess at first. If you go back and look at some early examples of C code, you'll be shocked at how sloppy the code looks. Years of collective experience developing, maintaining, and porting C code have taught us how to steer clear of many pitfalls. C++ will go through the same evolution. To sum up, pay attention or you'll turn into an antique!

Why Another C++ Book?

The problem with existing C++ books is that the language is difficult for beginners and so are the books. They seem to provide a compendium of complexities, overwhelming all but the stoutest of hearts and largest of craniums. We believe that C++ has crossed the *single book complexity barrier*. That's our own term: it means that the language is too complicated to fit into a single book. We compare learning C++ to learning physics. Nobody writing an introductory book on physics includes the general theory of relativity, except in the most superficial way. Instead students learn about Newtonian physics and get used to that, then move on to special relativity, get used to that, then on to general relativity.

We claim that C++ has gotten so complicated that it needs to be learned that way too. It's not that the sum of the complexity of the individual features is all that great. The problem is that when you put the features together they *interact* in highly nonintuitive ways. Consider this line from Page 330 of *The Design and Evolution of C++* by Bjarne Stroustrup, the designer of C++: "I think it was Martin O'Riordan who first brought this phenomenon [a surprising interaction between multiple inheritance and casting] to my attention." Think about this. Here's the author of the C++ language, a veteran of fifteen years of delving into every detail of the language, getting subtle interactions pointed out to him by someone else. Bjarne Stroustrup did a remarkable job of attaining his design goals for the language. They included such difficult real-world considerations as efficiency, compatibility with C and existing linkers, and allowing a wide variety of design styles. But meeting these goals required making certain sacrifices, and, unfortunately for the C++ beginner, avoidance of surprising interactions was sacrificed.

The C++ books we've seen generally fall into two camps. The books in one camp discuss all of the features of the complete C++ language without going too deeply into the interactions of those features. They don't admit up front that they're not giving important details, so they give readers the illusion that they understand the complete language. The first time these readers try to use some of the trickier features of C++, they're in for a painful surprise due to the interactions. The books in the other camp *do* try to give all the details of the interactions, but they can be overwhelming. Many a C++ neophyte has become terrified of the language after reading one of these books. It can be quite demoralizing to get hit with all those details of what can go wrong and everything you have to remember. This is unfortunate because learning C++ *can* be fun and is *definitely* worth the effort. You just need to approach it in a more user-friendly way.

Our Subset Solution

Our solution is to write a book that covers a subset of the features of C++. The subset consists of what we consider the core features of the language, without which it's just not C++, and a handful of others that make it a reasonably useful language. We've tried to avoid adding so much that we end up getting the confusing interactions that plague the full language. Beginning C++'ers can use this subset to get familiar with the basics of the language, while avoiding the frustrations common to anyone leaping into full C++ programming without appropriate preparation. Then, once you're comfortable with the basics, you can read any of several other books that provide a more complete picture. We think beginners will be far better equipped to get something useful out of those books after reading this one.

Our subset is not meant to be an industrial-strength programming language. We intend it to be part of a learning experience. It prepares beginners for learning the rest of the language and becoming industrial-strength programmers. It's not even meant to be an elegant subset, or necessarily to convey the elegance of C++.

Does it sound like we're trying to avoid complaints about why we didn't include this feature and how could we leave out that feature? We are. Selecting the subset was a painful process. The features tend to work closely together in a wide variety of applications. That's what leads to the surprising interactions, and that's what makes it hard to pull out any single feature. Like tugging on a loose thread from a sweater, the thread just keeps coming and coming. Where to make the cuts on the subset was a topic of battles between us right up to the final manuscript. Even though it's impossible to choose a subset that pleases everyone all the time, we hope we've chosen well enough to make learning C++ more enjoyable.

Why Use C++?

You can get into a lot of trouble with C++ if you aren't careful. Knowing that, why would you use C++? We find that when pushing the computer to its limit, we can write code more elegantly in C++. It allows you to centralize various tasks, the most typical being memory management. C can compete in run-time performance, but the code usually ends up looking pretty ugly. Other languages can compete in elegance, but usually with a significant run-time performance penalty. If fast, elegant code is important to you, then we recommend C++.

Organization of This Book

Chapter 1, *Object-Oriented Programming with Classes*, is a quick overview of OOP, which is the reason C++ was invented. We're not trying to teach OOP here. That's a topic for several books, not one chapter. But you only need the overview to understand this book.

Chapter 2, *C++ Without Classes*, describes some of the features of C++ that make general programming easier.

Chapter 3, *Abstraction with Member Functions*, presents the basics of classes. Classes are so central to C++ that the original version of C++ was called "C with Classes."

Chapter 4, *Encapsulation with Access Specifiers*, describes how to control access to the data and functions in classes.

Chapter 5, *Hierarchy with Composition and Derivation*, describes two powerful mechanisms for reusing code in C++.

Chapter 6, *Better Abstraction with Constructors and Destructors*, illustrates how to control the construction and destruction of objects.

Chapter 7, *Better Abstraction with new and delete*, describes the improved memory management mechanism C++ provides.

Chapter 8, *References*, answers the musical question, "When is a pointer not a pointer?"

Chapter 9, *Better Abstraction with Other Special Member Functions*, picks up where Chapter 6 leaves off describing special-purpose member functions.

Chapter 10, *An Example Class*, shows a few implementations of an example class using the special-purpose member functions from the previous chapter.

Chapter 11, *Better Hierarchy with Templates*, describes templates, which are like macros but safer and more powerful. If you're like us, you'll look at templates and think "what a hideous kludge." Then, after you use them for a while, you'll say "what an incredibly useful hideous kludge."

Chapter 12, *Polymorphism with Virtual Functions*, tells how to write code in C++ that is independent of the type of objects it is manipulating.

Chapter 13, *More About Polymorphism*, continues with more advanced features of polymorphism.

Chapter 14, *Implementing an Object-Oriented Design*, discusses the problems associated with implementing an object-oriented design.

Chapter 15, *An Example Program*, is an example program that demonstrates most of the features in our subset of C++.

Chapter 16, *What to Study Next*, suggests how to continue your C++ education.

Appendix A, *C++ Operators*, is for reference. It provides a complete list of all C++ operators and their precedence.

Appendix B, *One Problem with Returning by Value*, is a discussion of the problems of passing classes by value, as introduced in Chapter 8.

Finally, the book contains a bibliography of other useful books on C++.

Getting C++

C++ is popular enough that you can usually buy a compiler from the same place you got your hardware or the same place you usually buy software. If that doesn't work, or you want to check out other sources of C++, including freeware or shareware, try the resources listed in the bibliography. Magazines and the Internet are where to get the latest information and recommendations. We hesitate to supply them ourselves because both are quickly dated in this volatile market.

Obtaining Online Examples

The example programs in this book are available electronically in a number of ways: by FTP, *ftpmail*, BITFTP, and UUCP. The cheapest, fastest, and easiest ways are listed first. If you read from the top down, the first one that works for you is probably the best. Use FTP if you are directly on the Internet. Use *ftpmail* if you are not on the Internet, but can send and receive electronic mail to Internet sites (this includes CompuServe users). Use BITFTP if you send electronic mail via BIT-NET. Use UUCP if none of the above works.

FTP

To use FTP, you need a machine with direct access to the Internet. A sample session is shown, with what you should type in **boldface**.

```
% ftp ftp.uu.net
Connected to ftp.uu.net.
220 FTP server (Version 6.21 Tue Mar 10 22:09:55 EST 1992) ready.
Name (ftp.uu.net:joe): anonymous
331 Guest login ok, send domain style e-mail address as password.
Password: joe@ora.com (use your user name and host here)
230 Guest login ok, access restrictions apply.
ftp> cd /published/oreilly/nutshell/c.core
250 CWD command successful.
ftp> binary (You must specify binary transfer for compressed files.)
200 Type set to I.
ftp> get examples.tar.Z
200 PORT command successful.
150 Opening BINARY mode data connection for examples.tar.Z.
226 Transfer complete.
ftp> quit
221 Goodbye.
%
```

The file is a compressed *tar* archive; extract the files from the archive by typing:

```
% zcat examples.tar.Z | tar xvf -
```

System V systems require the following *tar* command instead:

```
% zcat examples.tar.Z | tar xof -
```

If *zcat* is not available on your system, use separate *uncompress* and *tar* or *shar* commands.

```
% uncompress examples.tar.Z
% tar xvf examples.tar.Z
```

ftpmail

ftpmail is a mail server available to anyone who can send electronic mail to, and receive it from, Internet sites. This includes any company or service provider that allows email connections to the Internet. Here's how you do it.

You send mail to *ftpmail@online.ora.com*. In the message body, give the FTP commands you want to run. The server will run anonymous FTP for you and mail the files back to you. To get a complete help file, send a message with no subject and the single word "help" in the body. The following is a sample mail session that should get you the examples. This command sends you a listing of the files in the selected directory and the requested example files. The listing is useful if there's a later version of the examples you're interested in.

```
% mail ftpmail@online.ora.com
Subject:
reply-to username@hostname.domainname        Where you want files mailed
open
cd /published/oreilly/nutshell/c.core
dir
mode binary
uuencode
get examples.tar.Z
quit
.
```

A signature at the end of the message is acceptable as long as it appears after "quit."

BITFTP

BITFTP is a mail server for BITNET users. You send it electronic mail messages requesting files, and it sends you back the files by electronic mail. BITFTP currently serves only users who send it mail from nodes that are directly on BITNET, EARN, or NetNorth. BITFTP is a public service of Princeton University. Here's how it works.

To use BITFTP, send mail containing your ftp commands to *BITFTP@PUCC*. For a complete help file, send HELP as the message body.

The following is the message body you send to BITFTP:

```
FTP   ftp.uu.net   NETDATA
USER  anonymous
PASS  myname@podunk.edu  Put your Internet email address here
                         (not your BITNET address)
```

```
CD  /published/oreilly/nutshell/c.core
DIR
BINARY
GET  examples.tar.Z
QUIT
```

Once you've got the desired file, follow the directions under FTP to extract the files from the archive. If you are not on a UNIX system, you may need to get versions of *uudecode, uncompress, atob,* and *tar* for your system. VMS, DOS, and Mac versions are available. The VMS versions are on *gatekeeper.dec.com* in */pub/VMS*.

Questions about BITFTP should go to Melinda Varian, *MAINT@PUCC* on BITNET.

UUCP

UUCP is standard on virtually all UNIX systems and is available for IBM-compatible PCs and Apple Macintoshes. The examples are available by UUCP via modem from UUNET; UUNET's connect-time charges apply.

You can get the examples from UUNET whether you have an account there or not. If you or your company has an account with UUNET, you have a system somewhere with a direct UUCP connection to UUNET. Find that system, and type (on one line):

```
uucp uunet\!~/published/oreilly/nutshell/c.core/examples.tar.Z
     yourhost\!~/yourname/
```

The backslashes can be omitted if you use the Bourne shell (*sh*) instead of *csh*. The file should appear some time later (up to a day or more) in the directory */usr/spool/uucppublic/yourname*. If you don't have an account, but would like one so that you can get electronic mail, contact UUNET at (703) 204-8000.

It's a good idea to get the file */published/oreilly/ls-lR.Z* as a short test file containing the filenames and sizes of all the files available.

Once you've got the desired file, follow the directions under FTP to extract the files from the archive.

Conventions

We use *italic font* for new key terms when they are defined, and for filenames when they appear in the body of a paragraph. We use `Courier font` (constant width) to show computer output and fragments of source code.

Acknowledgments

We would like to express our gratitude to Joe Pruett, Ward Cunningham, Ron Lunde, and Rob Daasch for their expert advice and support.

Thanks for the helpful feedback from our reviewers, Brian T. Hill, Paul Kleppner, Barbara J. Wagreich, André Alguero, David Cohen, Andrew Migliore, Jeff Yemin, Ken Dood, Dan Pasette, and Giao Tran. Special thanks to Stan Lippman.

We are grateful to Anne Pycha for her reviews, comments, and encouragement.

We thank our editor, Adrian Nye and all the people at O'Reilly & Associates who made this book a reality. These include Mary Anne Weeks Mayo, project manager/copyeditor for the book; Len Muellner and Ellen Siever, who converted the book from troff to SGML and contributed their tool-tweaking prowess; Chris Reilley, who created the excellent figures; Edie Freedman, who designed the cover; Nancy Priest, who designed the interior layout; Hanna Dyer, who designed the back cover; Seth Maislin, who prepared the index; Kismet McDonough-Chan, who did the final quality control on the book; and Michael Deutsch, who assisted with production.

Greg thanks Electronic Book Technologies and we both thank Summit Design for their support in writing this book while we were in their employ. Greg also thanks the Portland Pretzel Company for a friendly and tasty place to take breaks.

Finally, special thanks to the Jean DeMaiffe Courier Service for perfect deliveries.

In this chapter:
- *Object-Oriented Programming*
- *Classes*

Object-Oriented Programming with Classes

C++ extends the popular programming language C to support object-oriented programming. To understand C++, you must first understand object-oriented programming and what C++ adds to C to support this new way of programming. This chapter discusses both issues. First, we define object-oriented programming. Then, we introduce *classes*, the main C++ construct added to support object-oriented programming.

Object-Oriented Programming

Object-oriented programming (OOP) focuses on the *objects* that make up a program, rather than the functions and data. An object can represent some real-life concept like a car or a solar system. It could also represent something more abstract, like a stack of numbers or a sorting engine. Each object has a well-defined set of abilities. A car might be able to start, stop, and turn. A stack can have a value pushed on or popped off.

OOP consists of creating these objects and making them work together. You might use OOP to create a complete working program. Or you might supply a collection of objects that provide some service to others. The *user* (or *client*) of an object you create may be you, someone in your company, or someone you'll never meet.

You don't need an OOP language to program using objects; this can be done even in C. But a language like C++ makes OOP easier, because it directly supports the creation and use of objects.

To be more formal, OOP languages usually support a few key features. Every object philosopher includes a slightly different set. The ones we think most important are:

- Abstraction

- Encapsulation

- Hierarchy

- Polymorphism

Chances are you've used these programming concepts, perhaps under different names. We define each below, sometimes showing how they might be implemented in C.

Abstraction

Abstraction is the creation of a well-defined interface for an object. Proper abstraction separates the implementation of an object from its interface. In C, abstraction involves wrapping a data structure with a functional interface.

Let's say we need a stack of integers of some fixed maximum size. If we're not concerned with abstraction, we could use an array and access it directly:

```
main() {
    int stack_items[STACKSIZE], stack_top = 0, x;
    /* ... */
    stack_items[stack_top++] = x;  /* push onto the stack */
    /* ... */
    x = stack_items[--stack_top];  /* pop off the stack */
}
```

Here `stack_items` is an array holding a stack of integers whose top element is indicated by `stack_top`. We push `x` onto the stack and later pop a value off and place it in `x`.

The abstraction approach is to put a functional layer between the implementation of the stack and the code using it:

```
void init(Stack *s);        /* initialize the stack */
void push(Stack *s, int i); /* push an element onto the stack */
int  pop(Stack *s);         /* pop an element off the stack */
void cleanup(Stack *s);     /* clean up the stack when you're done with it */
```

These functions define the four abilities of our stack. The function `init()` sets up a new, empty stack. The function `push()` puts an element on top of the stack and `pop()` takes the top element off and returns it. We call `cleanup()` when we are done with the stack and it can be dismantled. Together these functions create the interface to our stack. Each of these functions takes a `Stack*` as its first parameter. `Stack` contains the data needed by the stack.

After declaring the functional interface, we can implement the underlying data and code:

```
typedef struct {
    int items[STACKSIZE];
    int top;
} Stack;

void init(Stack *s)          {s->top = 0;}
void push(Stack *s, int i) {s->items[s->top++] = i;}
int  pop(Stack *s)           {return s->items[--s->top];}
void cleanup(Stack *s)       {/* nothing for static stack */}
```

An instance of the struct Stack holds the stack's data. The user of a Stack instance passes this instance to each interface function. Notice that push() and pop() access the stack items just as in the nonabstraction version above.

Whenever we access the stack, we use the functional interface:

```
main() {
    int x;
    Stack stack1;
    /* ... */
    init(&stack1);
    /* ... */
    push(&stack1, x);
    /* ... */
    x = pop(&stack1);
    /* ... */
    cleanup(&stack1);
}
```

This example shows how calls to our functional interface replace direct manipulation of the data.

One advantage of astraction is that we've localized the code that manipulates the data. If we need to change the way we handle the data, we can change it in one place, rather than in all the places in our program that would otherwise access the data directly.

For example, we might start out with requirements that say the stack will never exceed some small size, so we can just allocate memory statically as in the example above. Then the requirements change, and we have to make the array grow when necessary. If we've abstracted, as we did in this example, these changes will be simple. Just change the type to use a dynamic array rather than a static one. The cleanup() function would then free the dynamic array. If we haven't abstracted, we have to find all the places where we access the array and change the code. This could get very messy.

Encapsulation

Encapsulation means keeping the implementation details of your abstractions private. The previous section explained that abstraction requires you to think carefully about an object's interface. The other aspect of deciding what the user should see is ensuring that that is *all* the user sees. Proper encapsulation both encourages and enforces the hiding of implementation details. It makes your code more reliable and easier to maintain because you know exactly what can be done with the abstractions you implement.

Encapsulation can take many forms. In some languages, it's impossible to access internal details. Other languages allow you to look at private information, but make it difficult enough that you won't do it accidentally.

In C, you keep details private by hiding them in a separate file. We can put the implementation of our Stack interface functions in its own file:

```
/* in stack.h: only the declarations (stack user sees these) */
void init(Stack *s);
void push(Stack *s, int i);
int pop(Stack *s);
void cleanup(Stack *s);

/* in stack.c: the definitions (stack user never sees these) */
void init(Stack *s) {s->top = 0;}
/* ... */
```

Here the file *stack.h* contains just the declarations of Stack's interface functions. We define them in *stack.c* where the Stack user cannot see. Furthermore, we can declare any functions that Stack needs privately to be static in this file.

Hiding Stack data requires us to be more tricky. We could use a stack ID and store the actual data in a separate code file:

```
/* in stack.h: the user sees only an ID */
typedef int Stack;

/* in stack.c: we store the stacks by stack ID */
struct {
    int items[STACKSIZE];
    int top;
} stacks[NUMSTACKS];
```

Here Stack is actually only an int. Inside the Stack code file, this int indexes an array called stacks that holds the actual data. Clearly this method creates a lot of work simply to hide our implementation. C++ drastically improves upon this primitive form of encapsulation.

Hierarchy

We can reuse a good abstraction as the basis of many other abstractions. In this way, we create powerful hierarchies of abstractions, one piece at a time. Our Stack abstraction uses an int and an int array. These simple abstractions might not seem too powerful, but by using them, we have created a useful new abstraction. Once we implement the Stack, we can use it as the basis of many other abstractions. Smart reuse can save a lot of time and energy.

The kind of hierarchy we've already seen—where one object uses others in its implementation—is called *composition* because we compose larger objects out of smaller ones. In the example above, the stack is composed of an int array to hold elements of the stack, and an int to hold the stack size. The other kind of hierarchy found in OOP languages is called *derivation* (or *inheritance*). Derivation allows an abstraction to reuse not only the implementation, but also the interface of another abstraction. For example, suppose we want to create another kind of stack that—in addition to the normal abilities—returns statistics like the mean, median, and mode of its elements. If we compose this StatStack from Stack we'd have to declare interface functions in StatStack that exist simply to call the corresponding ones in Stack:

```
typedef struct {
    Stack basic_stack;
} StatStack;

/* new to StatStack */
int mean(StatStack *s)    {/*...*/}
int median(StatStack *s)  {/*...*/}
int mode(StatStack *s)    {/*...*/}

/* in Stack */
void ss_init(StatStack *s)          {init(&s->basic_stack);}
void ss_push(StatStack *s, int i)   {push(&s->basic_stack, i);}
int  ss_pop(StatStack *s)           {return pop(&s->basic_stack);}
void ss_cleanup(StatStack *s)       {cleanup(&s->basic_stack);}
```

Here we have composed StatStack from a Stack. It has three functions—mean(), median(), and mode()—that return various statistics on the elements. It also has its version of functions like push() that already exist in Stack; these simply call the corresponding function on the basic_stack field.

It's a lot of work to repeat the interface of Stack in StatStack. Instead we really want StatStack to *inherit* the interface of Stack, so all we have to do is add the new functions. We want to be able to say something like:

```
StatStack is a Stack plus:
int mean(StatStack *s)    {/*...*/}
int median(StatStack *s) {/*...*/}
int mode(StatStack *s)    {/*...*/}
```

This is exactly what derivation allows us to say. It is possible to simulate derivation in C, but it's not common.

Polymorphism

Code is said to be polymorphic if it can be transparently used on instances of different types. The classic example is a group of classes representing different planar shapes: rectangles, ovals, etc. Each shape knows how to draw itself, calculate its area, and so on. Every type of shape does this differently, of course, but they all share these abilities. Polymorphism allows us to write code in terms of a generic shape type and have it work correctly for any actual shape. We'll discuss this more in Chapter 12, *Polymorphism with Virtual Functions*, and Chapter 13, *More About Polymorphism*.

What Are These Boxes?

You will see these *advanced-topic boxes* spread throughout the book. If we compare learning C++ to walking up a mountain trail, this book seeks to guide you up the most gradual path. Between Comment Canyon and Polymorphism Point, however, are many beautiful side trails with labels like Operator-Overloading Overlook and Friend-Function Forest. These trails are not for the beginner. Boxes like this serve as trail markers noting where other paths lie, and warning you away for now.

Of course, you will encounter these advanced topics in other books and other C++ code. We hope the explanations provided in these boxes will be enough to satisfy a beginning curiosity. Skip them as you read if you like; they are not necessary to understand this book. When you do read them, remember: we often cut a feature from our subset not because it is difficult to understand by itself, but because it interacts in complex ways with other parts of the language. These boxes only introduce each topic; they usually don't point out its subtleties or dangers.

Classes

Now that you have an idea of what OOP is, you are ready to see what C++ adds to C to support it. The fundamental addition is the *class*. A class describes the form and behavior of objects. It is like a stamp out of which you can press as many objects as you want.

Syntactically, a C++ class looks like a C struct. It contains a few straightforward additions that facilitate OOP. It is these additions we will study throughout the book. A class for a stack might look like this:

```
class Stack {              // class definition:
public:                    // access specifier
    void push(int i);      // member function
    int pop();
    Stack();               // instead of init()
    ~Stack();              // instead of cleanup()

private:                   // access specifier
    int items[STACKSIZE];  // data member
    int top;
};
```

This simple `Stack` class is similar to the struct with the same name that we showed earlier in the "Abstraction" section. Note, however, that the class contains the `Stack` interface functions (while the C version had them outside the `struct`). These *member functions* make abstraction much simpler to implement, as we'll see in Chapter 3, *Abstraction with Member Functions*. Also, the functions `init()` and `cleanup()` have been replaced with member functions `Stack()` and `~Stack()`. These special member functions get the compiler to handle object initialization and cleanup for you, as we'll see in Chapter 6, *Better Abstraction with Constructors and Destructors*. Next, the class contains the labels `public` and `private`. These *access specifiers* allow a flexible form of encapsulation, as we'll see in Chapter 4, *Encapsulation with Access Specifiers*. Finally, the *data members* support composition, the simpler form of hierarchy. The two advanced OOP concepts that we have not mentioned in this example—derivation and polymorphism—are supported by constructs we'll show later in the book.

Once you have defined a class, you use it like this:

```
main() {
    Stack s;
    /* ... */
    s.push(5);
    /* ... */
    i = s.pop();
    /* ... */
}
```

Here s is a Stack object. We declare it like we declare any variable. We then call
the various member functions on s, using syntax similar to that used with C
structs.

A class is essentially a new type you are adding to the programming language.
Once we implement the Stack class, we can use it much like we use the types that
come as part of the language. We call a class a *user-defined* type to differentiate it
from the *built-in* types that come with the language.

2

C++ Without Classes

The differences between C and C++ naturally divide into two groups. The first is a collection of improvements that you can understand without knowing object-oriented programming (OOP). The second consists of the additions that directly support OOP. We cover the first group in this chapter and the second group for the rest of the book. Because the major support for OOP in C++ is the class construct, we have dubbed this chapter's subset of the language "C++ Without Classes."

In this chapter, we first cover three features you will use constantly when writing C++ programs. Then, we discuss changes to help you manage all the function calls you'll be writing to implement your abstractions. After that we see some improvements that C++ makes to strengthen C's type system. Next, we show how in C++ you can initialize a global variable dynamically, that is, at run-time. Finally, we present a few lists that you might find helpful when you begin programming in C++.

Three to Start

This section contains three simple C++ features that you'll find handy. While not strictly necessary, they are so basic and useful that they alone make people want to use C++. You'll soon be wondering how you ever got by without them.

New-Style Comments

C++ adds a new kind of comment that begins with a double slash (//) and ends at
the end of the line:

```
/* this is a comment
   in C and C++ ending here -> */
int five = 2+2;    // this is a comment in C++ ending at the end of the line ->
```

The delimiter for one type of comment has no special meaning inside the other
type of comment:

```
/* comment ends here -> */
/* // comment still
   ends here -> */
// ... /* ... */ <- comment does NOT end here, but rather at end of line ->
```

New-style comments are most useful for short, one-line comments, like on a variable declaration. Old-style comments are still needed to comment out part of a
line. Personal preference determines when you should use either comment style.

struct, enum, and union Tags Are Type Names

In C, you must always prepend the keyword struct to a struct tag. For example,
we must write struct FooTag in this example:

```
/* C code */
struct FooTag {
    struct FooTag *next; /* keyword "struct" required */
    /* ... */
};
struct FooTag myfoo1;    /* here too */
FooTag myfoo2;           /* error: forgot "struct" */
```

The declaration of next and myfoo1 are correct; myfoo2's declaration requires the
keyword struct. In C++ you don't need to repeat the keyword struct once you
declare the struct tag:

```
// C++ code
struct Bar {        // struct tag Bar is declared at this point
    Bar *next;      // you needn't precede struct tag Bar with keyword "struct"
    // ...
};
struct Bar mybar1; // you can still write "struct Bar"
Bar mybar2;        // but you don't need to
```

Here, even though Bar is a struct tag, we can declare next and mybar2 using Bar
without the struct keyword. The declaration of mybar1 shows that you can still
use the keyword struct if you like.

We can do the same with enum tags:

```
enum Color {RED, WHITE, BLUE};
enum Color background;      /* in C we'd have to write this */
Color foreground;           // in C++ we can (and do) write this
```

and with union tags:

```
union Token_value {
    int ival;
    double dval;
    char *sval;
};
union Token_value token1;   /* must do this in C */
Token_value token2;         // can do this in C++
```

Of course, C programmers usually create these shorter names with typedefs. In fact, a struct is often defined as part of a typedef, so that we can give it a short name at the same time:

```
typedef struct {    /* in C, struct definition is usually part of typedef */
    Foo *head;
    Foo *tail;
} FooQueue;
```

Here we don't bother giving the struct a name, we just supply a short one with a typedef. In C++, this typedef is no longer needed. Dropping it, however, often causes even experienced C++ programmers to forget the semicolon that follows the struct definition:

```
struct FooQueue {    // in C++, typedef not needed
    Foo *head;
    Foo *tail;
}                    // <-- oops: forgot the semicolon after FooQueue definition
main() {/*...*/}     //          does main() return a FooQueue?
```

The definition of FooQueue needs to end with a semicolon. Without it, it looks like we are saying that main() returns an instance of this struct.

iostream: The New I/O Library

Like C, C++ has a standard I/O library, called the *iostream* library. C++ does not use C's *stdio* library for two main reasons. First, functions like printf() are not type-safe. It would be difficult for a compiler to determine that you are passing an instance of the wrong type to printf(). Second, *stdio* functions are not extensible. You cannot add your own type to printf()'s format string. In a later chapter we will show you how to extend the *iostream* library to print your own types. For now we concentrate on printing built-in types.

The most obvious feature of the *iostream* library is that it uses the shift operators instead of standard function calls. The classic first C program, for example, translates into this:

```
#include <iostream.h>
main() {
    cout << "hello, world\n";
}
```

This prints:

```
hello, world
```

to the standard output. To write to standard output, you use a variable called cout, declared in the *iostream* header, and the left-shift operator. When used for printing we'll call the left-shift operator the *printing operator*. The syntax is meant to suggest that you are sending data to cout. This is your first example of *operator overloading*, a new feature of C++ that allows you to give operators special meanings when they're used on your own types. In this case, the creator of the *iostream* library has overloaded the << operator for output.

You can print a value of any built-in type in this way:

```
cout << 22.0 / 7.0;     // prints a double
cout << 'x';            // prints a char
cout << (5 & 6);        // prints an int
```

The parentheses are needed in the final example, because << has a higher precedence than binary &. Operator overloading does not change the precedence of operators, only what types they work on.

A char* is expected to point to a null-terminated string. When you print a char*, this string is shown; all other pointers are printed as addresses:

```
char *s = "a fool, a tool, a pool: loopalootaloofa";
cout << s;              // prints the string
cout << (void *)s;      // prints the address of the string
```

You can print many values in one statement, like this code:

```
cout << "the sum of " << 3 << " and " << 4 << " is " << 3+4 << '\n';
```

which prints this output:

```
the sum of 3 and 4 is 7
```

The *iostream* library provides cerr to write to standard error. It is used like cout, but does not buffer its output.[*] The following function prints the square root of its

---

[*] Buffering speeds output by gathering a group of characters before actually printing them. It is not used by cerr so that debugging output messages appear promptly. The *c* in these

parameter to standard output. If the parameter is negative, however, it prints an error to standard error:

```
void print_sqrt(double d) {
    if (d >= 0) cout << "sqrt: " << sqrt(d) << '\n';
    else cerr << "negative number passed\n";
}
```

Though the syntax of printing with the *iostream* library is its most noticeable feature, this is only the beginning of its power. It is a flexible and complex library. You can find many C++ books that explain it in great detail. One book, listed in the Bibliography, is entirely devoted to it.

We are not going into the many features of the *iostream* library here. Specifically, we are not telling you how to format your output, how to read input, how to perform I/O on files and memory buffers, etc. If you need any of these features while learning our subset, use the C I/O library. It continues to work with C++.

If you want to use both libraries in the same program, you must call a special *iostream* function:

```
#include <stdio.h>          // C I/O library header
#include <iostream.h>       // C++ I/O library header
main() {
    ios::sync_with_stdio(); // call this function so iostream works with stdio

    cout << "now use iostream\n";
    printf("and stdio\n");
}
```

The function call `ios::sync_with_stdio()` allows you to freely mix the two libraries. This strange syntax, using two colons, will become clear in the next chapter.

Function Changes

Proper abstraction requires you to use function calls to hide implementations. To manage all the functions you'll use, C++ tightens the type requirements for functions. You must always declare a function, including its parameter types, before you use it. To allow flexibility, however, you can give two functions the same name as long as they can be distinguished by their parameters. This section discusses these changes.

---

variable names, by the way, stands for *character*. You can think of the *iostream* library as translating between objects and a stream of characters.

Function Declarations

A function *declaration* or *prototype* shows the interface to the function but not the function body. In C++ and ANSI/ISO C, function declarations look like this:

```
long foo(char *a);      // declaration of foo(): takes char*, returns long
float bar(int, char);   // declaration of bar(): takes int and char,
                        //                       returns float
```

They consist of the function name, parameter types, and return type. Parameter names are optional. A function *definition* includes the body of the function:

```
int next(int i) {return i+1;}    // definition of next()
```

A function *invocation* is a call to that function:

```
int main() {
    return next(5);    // invocation of next()
}
```

The declaration serves as a bridge that ties an invocation to its definition. In C, this bridge is optional; the compiler allows you to invoke a function that has not been declared (or actually defined) up to that point in the source code. In C++, a function must be declared (or actually defined) before it is invoked, or the compiler will complain. Requiring a declaration before an invocation allows the C++ compiler to catch common mistakes a C compiler might miss, like incorrect parameter types or misspelled function names.

C++ and C differ in how they specify empty and unchecked argument lists in a function declaration, as shown in Table 2-1.

Table 2-1: Declaring No Arguments and Unchecked Arguments in C and C++

Meaning	C	C++
Function takes no arguments	f(void)	f() or f(void)
Don't check arguments	f()	f(...)

In C, a function declared as f() can take any parameters. You specify an empty argument list by declaring the function f(void). In C++, these both mean an empty argument list. You specify unchecked parameters by declaring the function with an ellipsis, like f(...).

Flexibility with Parameters

 To relieve the burden of handling many function parameters, C++ provides three techniques for dropping parameters at various times. We have already mentioned that parameter names are optional in a function declaration, as is true in `foo()` below:

```
int foo(char *a); // these are equivalent declarations
int foo(char *);
```

You can also drop the name of a parameter in the function definition. This tells the compiler that you don't plan to use that parameter. Here the third parameter of `draw3dPoint()` is unused:

```
void draw3dPoint(int x, int y, int) { // third parameter has no name so the
    draw2dPoint(x, y);                 // compiler knows we won't use it
}
main() {draw3dPoint(1, 2, 7);}        // arg still required in invocation
```

The function `draw3dPoint()`, presumably temporarily, uses only its first two parameters and calls `draw2dPoint()`. We avoid compiler warnings saying that the third parameter is not used by not giving it a name. This technique is helpful in the early stages of program development, when many functions are just stubs.

Finally, a function can have default values for some parameters. You can drop parameters with default values from the function invocation. Here the last two parameters of `dist()` have default values:

```
double dist(int x1, int y1, int x2 = 0, int y2 = 0) { // last two parameters
    return sqrt(sqr(x2-x1)+sqr(y2-y1));                // have default values
}

main() {
    double d1 = dist(1, 2, 3, 4);   // get dist between (1, 2) and (3, 4)
    double d2 = dist(1, 2, 3);      // get dist between (1, 2) and (3, 0)
    double d2 = dist(1, 2);         // get dist between (1, 2) and (0, 0)
}
```

The function `dist()` takes four parameters and returns the Euclidean distance between the two planar points they indicate. The last two parameters default to zero; we may supply fewer than four arguments when invoking the function, as we do when we initialize d2 ad d3.

Function Overloading

A function's *signature* is its name plus the number and types of the parameters it takes. Here is the declaration of a function named foo:

```
void foo(int a, char b);
```

Its signature is foo(int, char). C++ allows more than one function with the same name as long as their signatures differ:

```
void foo(int a, int b);      // first foo
void foo(int a);             // second foo
void foo(double a);          // third foo

main() {
    foo(1, 2);      // calls the first foo
    foo(1);         // calls the second foo
    foo(.5);        // calls the third foo
    // ...
}
```

Linkage

 C++ is designed to work with traditional linkers. Traditional linkers only know about a function's name, not its parameter types. So they cannot check that you passed the correct parameters, and they don't understand overloading. To solve these problems, C++ changes function names into function signatures before passing them to the linker. This is called *name encoding* or *name mangling*. You might get a glimpse of this if you call a function with the wrong arguments or forget to include the definition of an overloaded function. The linker may say something like this:

```
undefined symbol: func__FPi3Foo
```

This might be the encoding of the function func(int *, Foo).

C++ allows you to turn off name encoding so you can link to code compiled by a C compiler. This is done with a special extern declaration:

```
extern "C" int func(int *, Foo);
```

This function gets passed to the linker without having its parameter types encoded in its name.

This example shows three functions named `foo` with different signatures. When the compiler sees an invocation of `foo()`, it chooses the correct function based on the number and type of arguments listed. A name used by more than one function is said to be *overloaded*. Note that the return type is not part of the signature; you cannot overload two functions that are the same except for return type, like these two:[*]

```
void foo(int a, int b);      // first foo
double foo(int a, int b);    // error: same signature as first foo
```

When the number and type of arguments in a function invocation match some function signature exactly, there is no question about which function is called. If they do not match exactly, the compiler tries to do automatic casting to make the invocation match some function signature. Automatic casting can get quite complicated and subtle. For example:

```
void bar(double d);    // first bar
void bar(long l);      // second bar
main () {
    bar(3);            // ambiguous because 3 is an int
    // ...
}
```

In the example above, the argument in the invocation `bar(3)` is an `int`, which doesn't exactly match either the `double` or `long`. The compiler has to decide which is a "closer" match. In this particular case, the compiler will decide that neither is sufficiently closer and call this invocation an error.

We recommend making your arguments match exactly, adding more overloaded functions if necessary. It's better to avoid casts because they can be dangerous, but if you're careful with them they're still better than letting the compiler guess what automatic conversions to try. Here we have made each call to `bar()` match exactly one definition:

```
main() {
    int i;
    bar(3.0);          // calls first bar because 3.0 has type double
    bar(3L);           // calls second bar because 3L has type long
    bar((long)i);      // calls second bar because of cast
    // ...
}
```

---

[*] This restriction makes life easier for compiler writers. It is not always easy to determine what type a function invocation is expected to return. The compiler might have to analyze some arbitrarily large expression, for example.

Stricter Typing

In addition to strengthening the typing rules for functions, C++ has a number of small changes that strengthen the type system in other ways. Stricter typing allows C++ compilers to catch many bugs that would cause run-time problems in C. The goal of the changes discussed in this section is to prevent type ambiguities and accidental violations of the type system. C++ still lets you use casts to freely circumvent these rules. C++ prevents implicit, rather than explicit, type violations.

const

 The keyword const denotes a value that cannot be modified:

```
const int stone = 5;       // stone can never be modified
int strlen(const char *s); // strlen() will not modify
                           // what s points to
```

This is an extremely handy addition to the type system you may already use in C. Using const, you can enlist the compiler's help to make sure certain values do not change. Unfortunately for the C++ beginner, the meaning of const in C++ differs slightly from that of C. const can also be quite subtle and complicated to use correctly in C++. We think using const can get in the way of learning the basics. For these reasons, we leave const to a more advanced book. const should not be hard for you to use once you know the basics.

void: The Generic Pointer*

Like C, C++ allows you to implicitly convert a pointer to a void*:

```
void *v;
Foo *f;
v = f;             // implicit conversion to void*: ok in C and C++
```

We can assign f, a Foo*, to v, a void*, without a cast in both C and C++. C also allows you to implicitly convert a void* to other pointers. In C++, you need an explicit cast:

```
f = v;         // error in C++, ok in C: implicit conversion from void*
f = (Foo *)v;  // ok in C++ and C: explicit cast from void*
```

C++ requires a cast to assign v to f because a conversion from a void* is unsafe and implicit violations of the type system are dangerous. Fortunately, C++ removes the need for `void*` in many situations, as you will see later in the book. (For example, `malloc()` returns a `void*`, but this function is normally not used in C++, as we'll see in Chapter 7, *Better Abstraction with new and delete*.)

0: The Null Pointer

In C and C++, 0 in a pointer context represents the *null pointer.*[*] Here 0 is used as an `int` and as the null pointer:

```
int i = 0;      // i now contains the integer zero
char *s = 0;    // s now contains the null pointer
```

To make their intentions clear, most C programmers use the null-pointer macro `NULL` when they mean the null pointer:

```
/* C code */
#define NULL (void *)0    /* typical definition of null-pointer macro */
Foo *x = NULL;            /* works fine in C */
```

The macro `NULL` includes the `void*` cast so that it is always interpreted as a pointer rather than an integer, especially during function calls. But, in C++, as stated in the previous section, a `void*` cannot be assigned to an arbitrary pointer without a cast. If you want to use `NULL` in C++, without having to cast it each time, it must be defined simply as 0:

```
// C++ code
#define NULL 0    // most reasonable definition of null-pointer macro in C++
Foo *x = NULL;    // works fine in C++
```

Using 0 without a cast to `void*` works well in C++ because the context usually makes it clear whether you mean an integer or a pointer. In fact, many C++ programmers have dropped the macro and just use 0 in their code as the null pointer:

```
int *p = 0;    // many C++ programmers avoid NULL
```

Other programmers are reluctant to drop a favorite macro. We use 0 in this book because this has become standard in C++. Be prepared to see `NULL` or 0 in other programmers' code.

One good reason to be wary of `NULL` is that it causes problems, when an overloaded function can take an `int` or a pointer. The compiler thinks 0 matches an `int` better than a pointer:

```
#define NULL 0
void snafu(int i);      // first snafu
void snafu(char *c);    // second snafu
```

---

* Don't think of this 0 as an address. The null pointer need not actually be implemented as address 0, though it often is.

```
main() {
    snafu(0);              // danger: calls first snafu
                           //          this is not what you meant if you were using
                           //          0 as the null pointer
    snafu(NULL);           // error: calls first snafu
                           //          this is almost certainly not what you meant
}
```

These two invocations of snafu() both call snafu(int). It's best not to overload functions so that pointers and integers can get confused, unless you're never going to call them with the null pointer. If you can't avoid it, then a cast can make it clear:

```
void snafu(int i);         // first snafu
void snafu(char *c);       // second snafu

main() {
    snafu((int)0);         // calls first snafu, the cast is unnecessary,
                           //     but makes your intention clear
    snafu((char *)NULL);   // calls second snafu, the cast is essential
    // ...
}
```

Here we have added casts to tell the compiler which snafu() to invoke.

Character Literals Have Type char

In C, a character literal, such as 'a', has type int. This fact comes as a surprise to many C programmers, which shows that int works fine in C. In C++, character literals having type int doesn't work well with function overloading:

```
void print(int i);     // prints number
void print(char c);    // prints character
main() {
    print('a');            // we want this to call print(char)
}
```

We want the call print('a') to invoke print(char). For this reason, character literals evaluate to char in C++.

enums Are Distinct from ints

C++ strengthens the typing of enumerated types. You can no longer assign an integer to an enum variable without a cast:

```
enum Herb {Parsley, Sage, Rosemary, Thyme};
Herb h1 = 2;           // allowed in C, type violation in C++
Herb h2 = (Herb)2;     // allowed in C and C++
```

The assignment h1 = 2 is illegal in C++; a cast tells the compiler not to complain. You can still use enumerated type values where an integral value is expected in C++:

```
int i = Sage;        // allowed
char a[Thyme];       // allowed, but not necessarily recommended
```

Dynamic Initialization of Globals

Many of the changes discussed so far take the form of restrictions that increase type safety. This section shows a change that *adds* flexibility rather than removing it. In C, only a constant expression can initialize a global variable. C++ removes this restriction:

```
int global1 = 3;           // static init of global: ok in C and C++
int global2 = my_func();   // dynamic init of global: error in C, ok in C++
float global3 = global2 * 2.0; // dynamic init of global: error in C, ok in C++
main() {/*...*/}
```

The initialization of global1 is *static*; it is complete at compile-time. The other two initializations are *dynamic*; they must be deferred until run-time. These last two initializations are not allowed in C; they are in C++. This added power raises two questions: when and in what order are these globals dynamically initialized?

Globals are typically dynamically initialized before main() is entered. No longer is main() necessarily the first piece of your code that runs. In the example above, my_func() executes during the initialization of global2 before main() runs. Keep this in mind when your program crashes without reaching the breakpoint you set at the beginning of main(). Because the compiler may actually insert some code to dynamically initialize globals into the beginning of main(), C++ forbids overloading, calling, or taking the address of main().

Within a translation unit, globals are dynamically initialized in the order they are defined.[*] Between translation units, the order of dynamic initialization is undefined. This only causes problems if one global depends on another in a separate translation unit. For example, if global2 and global3 above were in different translation units, there is no guarantee that global2 would be properly initialized before its value is needed by global3.

The simple solution is to not initialize globals with other globals or only with globals defined in the same translation unit. This is not always easy to ensure, because the dependency can be indirect. The function my_func() initializing global2 above,

---

* A *translation unit* is the basis of a C++ compilation. It is a source file after preprocessing is complete. Remember that extern globals can be *declared* in many different translation units, but *defined* in only one.

for example, could require some other global to already be dynamically initialized. You typically don't need to worry about this when using globals—like cout and cerr—from a library. Library writers can employ nifty tricks to ensure library globals are initialized before they are used.

Some Final Lists

Before we leave this chapter, we cover a few final details of the language. You can refer to the lists that follow as you begin writing C++ programs.

File Suffixes

There is no single convention for the suffix to use for a C++ code file. Possibilities include .C, .cc, .cp, .cpp, .cxx, and .c++. The suffix for a C++ header file is typically analogous: .H, .hh, etc. Many programmers continue to use .h, however. Make your choice based on local convention and what your compiler vendor uses.

Keywords and Identifiers

C++ has many new keywords. Make sure you do not use them as identifiers, that is, as the name of a variable, parameter, function, type, etc. This section lists all the keywords, divided into four handy categories.

The following keywords are ones you know and love from C:

auto	const	double	float	int	short	struct	unsigned
break	continue	else	for	long	signed	switch	void
case	default	enum	goto	register	sizeof	typedef	volatile
char	do	extern	if	return	static	union	while

The following keywords are new to C++:

asm	class	delete	new	private	public	throw	try
catch	friend	inline	operator	protected	this	template	virtual

A few of these keywords may be familiar to you because some C compilers have borrowed them. Also, in our experience, new is the keyword a beginner is most likely to try to use as an identifier. The following keywords are so new to C++ that they might not be recognized by your compiler yet:

bool	explicit	namespace	true	using
const_cast	false	reinterpret_cast	typeid	wchar_t
dynamic_cast	mutable	static_cast	typename	

You may remember wchar_t as a standard typedef in C. Finally, the following keywords are alternative representations for certain C++ operators. They facilitate C++ programming with character sets that lack characters needed by C++. These are also very new to C++:

and	bitand	compl	not_eq	or_eq	xor_eq
and_eq	bitor	not	or	xor	

To avoid clashing with names used by the compiler, linker, or standard libraries, don't start an identifier with an underscore or include a double underscore in an identifier:

```
this_is_fine_
_avoid_starting_with_underscore
avoid_double__underscores
```

This is overly cautious, but it will keep you out of trouble.

3

Abstraction with Member Functions

Now that you have seen an overview of object-oriented programming (OOP) and classes, we can explain exactly how C++ classes support OOP. In this chapter, we show how classes support abstraction by providing *member functions*. Recall that abstraction is the creation of a well-defined interface for an object. To demonstrate how to use a class to implement an abstraction, we show an example using a C struct and transform that example to use a C++ class.

The Abstraction

A good first example of abstraction is to add a more powerful array to C++. C++, like C, has minimal support for arrays. For example, even though we think of an array as having some fixed size, the built-in array does not store its size, nor does it check if an index is out of bounds. And even though we think about arrays as distinct from pointers, the language barely distinguishes between them. The array support provided by the language is mostly just convenient memory management and pointer arithmetic.[*]

This low-level array makes C++ quite flexible. You can use C++'s built-in array to create just the data structure needed, and the compiler does not add unrequested data or code. When done right, this can result in fast and efficient programs.

If speed of code were the only important metric, however, this would be a book on assembly-language programming. Object-oriented languages sacrifice some

---

[*] Perhaps the best evidence is that the brackets operator is, surprisingly, commutative. That is, if a is an array, a[5] and 5[a] are interchangeable. The brackets are just a shorthand for pointer arithmetic: a[5] = *(a+5) = *(5+a) = 5[a].

speed of execution for speed of development and maintenance. As computers get faster and the cost of software engineering rises, the importance of these factors increases rapidly.

In this chapter, we'll build several versions of an improved array that addresses the shortcomings of built-in arrays. To keep the example simple, we create an array of integers. In Chapter 11, *Better Hierarchy with Templates*, you will see how to generalize this example to an array of any type.

Using a struct

The simplest way to implement our proposed array is to wrap all of the needed data in a single struct. We'll do that in this section and see how it works.

Definition of struct

Our new array, which we're calling IntArray, looks like this:

```
// basing IntArray on plain struct
struct IntArray {
    int *elems;          // elements of array
    size_t numElems;     // number of elements in array
};
```

This IntArray struct packages a pointer to a built-in array and a count of the number of elements in the array. This takes care of our complaint that built-in arrays do not store their size.

The type size_t is defined in the standard header *stddef.h*. It is a typedef of the smallest unsigned type large enough to hold the result of sizeof, typically unsigned int or unsigned long. So numElems is large enough to hold the number of elements in the array, but no larger than necessary.

Use of struct

We now have a wrapper, IntArray, that represents our new array. We use it like this:

```
// using plain struct
main() {
    IntArray powersOf2 = {0, 0};    // holds some powers of two
    // ...
    powersOf2.numElems = 8;
    powersOf2.elems = (int *)malloc(powersOf2.numElems * sizeof (int));
    powersOf2.elems[0] = 1;
    powersOf2.elems[1] = 2 * powersOf2.elems[0];
    powersOf2.elems[2] = 2 * powersOf2.elems[1];
    // ...
```

```
        free(powersOf2.elems);
    }
```

In the first line of the main(), we create an instance of—or *instantiate*—the IntArray struct. We then use the instance, powersOf2, to hold our data. When done with this object, we must free the space allocated to hold the array elements.

In this example we write directly to and read directly from the fields of powersOf2. But an object's data is part of its implementation. If we allow direct access to the data, we can't guarantee it will be used correctly. For example, even though we've created a numElems field to store the number of elements, we still haven't provided a means of ensuring that an index is within bounds or even that the user sets this field correctly. A plain struct does not give the control we'd like over IntArray instances. In the next section, we take a step toward a more robust solution.

Using a struct with Interface Functions

To avoid direct and uncontrolled data access, we can make the user go through interface functions to interact with our objects. Interface functions provide the control necessary to make sure that our objects are used correctly. We modify IntArray to use interface functions in this section.

Declaration of Interface Functions

Here are the declarations of the interface functions to our IntArray objects:

```
// interface functions for our IntArray:
// create and destroy instances of IntArray
void IA_init(IntArray *object);
void IA_cleanup(IntArray *object);

// access the number of elements of the IntArray
void IA_setSize(IntArray *object, size_t value);
size_t IA_getSize(IntArray *object);

// access individual elements of the IntArray
void IA_setElem(IntArray *object, size_t index, int value);
int IA_getElem(IntArray *object, size_t index);
```

To indicate that these functions form the interface to IntArray objects and to prevent name clashes with another object's interface functions, we prefix each name with IA_. Furthermore, each function takes an object parameter of type IntArray*. This parameter is the object the function acts upon. In the language of OOP, these functions provide a means for users to request that an object perform some action on itself.

The first two functions perform basic housekeeping: the IA_init() function, for example, lets users of the IntArray class put an array into a known initial state, probably having no elements; the IA_cleanup() function lets users free the memory an array has allocated during its lifetime. The remaining functions allow users controlled access to the array's data: IA_setSize() sets the number of elements in the array and allocates storage for those elements; IA_getSize() returns the current number of elements in the array; finally, IA_setElem() and IA_getElem() access the individual elements.

This completes the declaration of the basic functions. We could dream up a wealth of useful functions to add: one to resize the array without losing information, one to sort the elements, and so on. But it's usually best to start with the core functions and add more as needed.

Definition of Interface Functions

Now we need to create definitions for all the interface functions we declared in the previous section. First, let's implement the initialization function:

```
// defining IA_init()
void IA_init(IntArray *object) {
    object->numElems = 0;
    object->elems = 0;
}
```

This function puts a new IntArray, passed in the object parameter, into an initial state with no elements. Now, let's implement the function to change the size of the array:

```
// defining IA_setSize()
void IA_setSize(IntArray *object, size_t value) {
    if (object->elems != 0) free(object->elems);
    object->numElems = value;
    object->elems = (int *)malloc(value * sizeof(int));
}
```

First we free the old elements, then we store the new number of elements and allocate space for them. Note that we could optimize this code by only reallocating when the size increases, but we've chosen to keep the implementation simple for now. Finally, let's implement the function to access a single element at a given index:

```
// defining IA_getElem()
int IA_getElem(IntArray *object, size_t index) {
    if (index >= object->numElems) error("bad index");    // doesn't return
    return object->elems[index];
}
```

This function shows that we have fulfilled our other design goal: our IntArray checks that an index is in range. To keep the code simple, we assume that error-reporting function error() does not return. We might want to make the error handling more sophisticated later, but this is good enough for now. Once we define the other three interface functions—which are similar to the three shown—we have implemented an IntArray using a struct and interface functions.

Use of Interface Functions

Let's redo our previous example in which we used the IntArray:

```
// using struct with interface functions
main() {
    IntArray powersOf2;      // holds some powers of two
    IA_init(&powersOf2);
    // ...
    IA_setSize(&powersOf2, 8);
    IA_setElem(&powersOf2, 0, 1);
    IA_setElem(&powersOf2, 1, 2 * IA_getElem(&powersOf2, 0));
    IA_setElem(&powersOf2, 2, 2 * IA_getElem(&powersOf2, 1));
    // ...
    IA_cleanup(&powersOf2);
}
```

Instead of directly accessing the data, we interact with the IntArray object only through its interface functions. We can now be sure that the size of the array is always correct, and we'll get an error if we try to access an element out of range.

Concerns About Interface Functions

You might worry about code size and speed, using functions to access an array. You could be tempted to access the data directly because you know how the object is implemented and want the extra speed. Or you might want to use #defines in place of functions. Don't worry about efficiency at this point. Rest assured that C++ provides a mechanism for avoiding the overhead of many small function calls.

You might also worry that deciding on the right interface functions will take a lot of time; this is true. Abstraction requires you to spend more time designing your interface. This initial investment is paid back many times by the ease of use of each new abstraction.

Finally, you might worry that the code is just longer and harder to understand. We've turned a simple array access into a mess of function calls. C++ has a number of mechanisms that address this syntactic issue. The next section shows one.

inline Functions

 Proper abstraction requires us to make many function calls instead of accessing the data directly. At the same time, programmers require—one might say C programmers demand—code that is as efficient as possible. To bridge this gap, C++ allows you to declare a function `inline`. Declaring a function `inline` is a hint to the compiler that the function should be expanded inline, like a macro. It looks like this:

```
inline int IA_getElem(IntArray *object, size_t index) {/*same code*/}
```

If the body of `IA_getElem` is simple enough, the compiler translates invocations of this function into direct data access. Because they are expanded by the compiler rather than the preprocessor, `inline` functions are more powerful than macros.

Using a Class with Member Functions

The `IntArray` implementation in the previous section consists of two basic pieces: the data holding the object's information and the functions making up the object's interface. Let's compare how the language handles these two pieces.

We have grouped the data together nicely using a struct. The struct is a powerful language feature for grouping related data. It results in shorter and clearer code because you can handle all the pieces of data at the same time. In addition, the names of a struct's fields are simple because they need only be unique within the struct. Finally, the compiler handles the data as a whole, increasing possibilities for optimization.

The interface functions have nothing but our `IA_` naming convention grouping them together or connecting them to the `IntArray` struct. But it is the data and functions together that create a whole object. C++ recognizes this relationship by allowing us to group data and functions together using a class. As you will see in later chapters, the ability to define class members that are functions is the basis of many OOP features. In this section we change our `IntArray` struct into a class, incorporating both the data and the interface functions.

First, let's recall what we came up with in the previous section. We used a struct and interface functions:

```
// recall the struct with interface functions from last section:
// data
struct IntArray {
```

```
        int *elems;
        size_t numElems;
};

// interface functions
void    IA_init(IntArray *object);
void    IA_cleanup(IntArray *object);
void    IA_setSize(IntArray *object, size_t value);
size_t  IA_getSize(IntArray *object);
void    IA_setElem(IntArray *object, size_t index, int value);
int     IA_getElem(IntArray *object, size_t index);
```

Here is the same example using a class. Notice how the functions are declared within the body of the class. Notice, too, that these functions have no IA_ prefix or object parameter:

```
// defining the same object as class with member functions
class IntArray {
public:
    void    init();
    void    cleanup();
    void    setSize(size t value);
    size_t  getSize();
    void    setElem(size_t index, int value);
    int     getElem(size_t index);

private:
    int *elems;
    size_t numElems;
};
```

In C++ parlance, elems and numElems are called *data members* of the IntArray class. The functions are called *member functions* of the IntArray class. We call the data and functions collectively *class members.*[*]

The public and private labels control access to the class members. We will discuss them in Chapter 4, *Encapsulation with Access Specifiers*. Ignore them for now.

The compiler does not care about the order of class member declarations. Note that we put the member functions first and the data members last. We order them like this to highlight that an object's interface is its most important piece: you should access the data only through the object's interface. In fact, you should not think about data at all until you have decided just what an object should be able to do.

---

* Other languages call data members *instance variables* and member functions *methods*. Why the word *member* goes after *data* but before *function* we do not know. We can only guess that someone found *function member* ambiguous and *member datum* silly. This non-parallel naming can be confusing.

Member Function Declaration

Now, let's take a closer look at member function declaration by comparing it with our earlier interface functions. When we create the interface functions for the IntArray struct, we prefaced the name of each function with IA_. Each function also took a first object parameter. The declarations looked like this:

```
// BEFORE: declaration of interface functions
struct IntArray {/*...*/};
// ...
void   IA_setSize(IntArray *object, size_t value);
size_t IA_getSize(IntArray *object);
// ...
```

When we created the member functions in the IntArray class, the IA_ prefix is gone and so is the object parameter:

```
// AFTER: declaration of member functions
class IntArray {
public:
    // ...
    void   setSize(size_t value);
    size_t getSize();
    // ...
};
```

You declare member functions within the class' curly braces. We have dropped the IA_ prefix from the function names because the functions, like the data, now only need their names to be unique within the class. So we no longer need a special naming scheme to prevent clashes. We have also dropped the initial object parameter from each function, because the compiler takes care of this parameter for us now that we have tied the functions and the data together. You will learn more about this below.

Member Function Invocation

Before we show how to define member functions, let's skip ahead and show how they are invoked. Here's how we used interface functions to create and manipulate an array in C:

```
// BEFORE: invoking interface functions
main() {
    IntArray powersOf2;
    IA_init(&powersOf2);
    // ...
    IA_setSize(&powersOf2, 8);
    IA_setElem(&powersOf2, 0, 1);
```

```
        IA_setElem(&powersOf2, 1, 2 * IA_getElem(&powersOf2, 0));
        // ...
        IA_cleanup(&powersOf2);
    }
```

Here's how we invoke member functions in C++:

```
    // AFTER: invoking member functions
    main() {
        IntArray powersOf2;
        powersOf2.init();
        // ...
        powersOf2.setSize(8);
        powersOf2.setElem(0, 1);
        powersOf2.setElem(1, 2 * powersOf2.getElem(0));
        // ...
        powersOf2.cleanup();
    }
```

This code shows that we call member functions much like we access the field of a struct: with the *dot operator*. Only the parentheses at the end show that these are member function calls. The second line of main(), for example, calls the init() member function on the powersOf2 object. Or, to use some OOP terminology, it sends a message to the powersOf2 object, telling it to initialize itself.

We can also invoke member functions through pointers to objects. This code example is similar to the one we just looked at, but it uses the standard pointer syntax:

```
    // accessing member functions through pointer to class instance
    main() {
        IntArray powersOf2;
        IntArray *ppow = &powersOf2;
        ppow->init();
        // ...
        ppow->setSize(8);
        ppow->setElem(0, 1);
        ppow->setElem(1, 2 * ppow->getElem(0));
        // ...
        ppow->cleanup();
    }
```

Pointers to objects play an important role in polymorphism as we'll see in Chapter 12, *Polymorphism with Virtual Functions*.

Member Function Definition

The declaration and invocation of member functions is pretty straightforward, but learning how to define them takes more time. We'll use getElem() as an example.

Here's what our function definition looked like before we packaged it with the class:

```
// BEFORE: definition of interface function
struct IntArray {/*...*/};
int IA_getElem(IntArray *object, size_t index) {
    if (index >= object->numElems) error("bad index");
    return object->elems[index];
}
```

And here's what the function definition looks like after we package it with the class:

```
// AFTER: definition of member function
class IntArray {/*...*/};
int IntArray::getElem(size_t index) {
    if (index >= this->numElems) error("bad index");
    return this->elems[index];
}
```

Though they are *declared* inside the class' curly braces, member functions are *defined* outside, like the interface functions were. There are two differences between the interface functions with the struct and the member functions with the class:

- The `IA_` prefix has mutated into an `IntArray::` prefix using a new double-colon syntax.

- The `object` pointer has been dropped as a parameter and replaced within the body of the function by the `this` pointer.

We cover both of these features in the following sections.

Defining Member Functions Inside a Class

Member functions can actually be defined when they are declared inside the class. This is sometimes done for short member functions, like this:

```
class Interjection {
    void happy() {cout << "hooray\n";}      // defined inside class
    void sad();                             // defined outside class
};
```

The scope operator ::

The first difference between the definition of a struct interface function and class member function is that IntArray:: prefixes the name of the member function. This prefix tells the compiler that we are defining an IntArray member function. Or, more formally, this prefix indicates the *scope* of the function we are defining. The scope of any identifier (for example, the name of a local variable) is the section of the program in which that identifier is known.

Block-structured languages consist of a series of nested scopes. In C, every function has *global scope*. A variable can have global scope, the scope of a function, or the scope of a block within a function. A field of a struct has the scope of that struct. That is, to refer to the field, the identifier must be prefixed by a variable of that struct's type.

Just as a struct field is known only within the struct that contains it, a member function is known only within the class that contains it. When we define an IntArray member function, for example, the IntArray:: prefix is necessary because we define the function outside of the class' braces. The double colon is called the *scope operator* because it is used to specify the scope from which an identifier comes. Without this prefix, this would be the definition of a regular function.[*] With the prefix, we are telling the compiler that even though lexically this function definition is not inside the class, logically it is.

Global Scope Operator

Even regular functions can have their scope shown explicitly. They are said to exist in the *global scope*, which is indicated with the *global scope operator*. This is just the standard scope operator with no class on its left:

```
#include <string.h>         // declares strlen()
main() {
    int strlen;             // hides global name strlen
    // ...
    strlen = ::strlen("hello?"); // use global scope
                                 // operator to get strlen()
    // ...
}
```

Here we access the standard function strlen() with its scope operator because we have hidden it with a local variable having the same name.

---

[*] Also called a *global* or *non-member* function.

This prefix is necessary to uniquely identify the function. We can drop it, however, when the class is clear. For example, we do not use the prefix when the function is invoked, because the type of the object on which the function is invoked determines which function we mean. In our discussions, we also drop the class prefix when the function to which we are referring is clear.

The this pointer

The second difference between the definition of a struct interface function versus that of a class member function is the omission of the object parameter. Instead, numElems and elems are accessed through a pointer called this. To what object does this refer? Inside a member function, the keyword this points to the object on which the member function was invoked. So, if the user calls:

```
foo.getElem(4);
```

then this points to foo, that is, this is equivalent to &foo. So in the definition of getElem(), repeated here:

```
// repeating definition of getElem()
int IntArray::getElem(size_t index) {
    if (index >= this->numElems) error("bad index");
    return this->elems[index];
}
```

the first line of the member function body accesses the numElems data member for the same object for which getElem() was called. The this pointer is used as if each member function had a hidden parameter called this of the correct type. The one restriction is that you may not change the value of this.[*]

Class scope allows dropping this

Above we said that member functions exist in class scope. So far, this has bought us simple naming of member functions and a hidden parameter handled by the compiler. The compiler does one other piece of bookkeeping for us: it keeps track of class members, so we do not need to prefix them with this. Inside a member function, class members not prefixed by an object refer to the object on which the member function was invoked. Thus, we can rewrite the above example as:

```
// dropping the this pointer
int IntArray::getElem(size_t index) {
    if (index >= numElems) error("bad index");
    return elems[index];
}
```

---

[*] The word *this* is an odd choice for a keyword. It is perhaps the first definite article to have this honor. Other languages use words like *self* or *me*.

Other Class Members

Classes were added to C++ to group together data and functions to form a blueprint for objects. The data members define the contents of every class instance and the member functions act on these class instances. This grouping ability of the class has proven so useful, however, that classes can contain more than just regular data members and member functions. Here's a class containing some of the variety:

```
class Foo {                    // a class with different kinds of members:
public:
    class Bar {/*...*/};       // a nested class
    typedef int myInt;         // a typedef
    enum {RED, BLUE, GREEN};   // enumeration constants
    static int staticDataMem;  // a static data member
    static void staticMemFunc(); // a static member function
};
```

The class `Foo` contains two types: a nested class called `Bar` and a `typedef` called `myInt`. It also contains three enumeration constants. We access the `enum`s and types with the scope operator:

```
main() {
    Foo::myInt myColor = Foo::BLUE;    // myColor is now an int with value 1
    // ...
}
```

The final two class members are a data member and a member function declared with the `static` keyword. A static data member like `staticDataMem` exists once for the whole class, not in each individual class instance. Adding one to a class does not increase the size of the class instances. A static member function like `staticMemFunc()` is not called on a particular class instance; it has no `this` pointer. Static members are accessed like this:

```
main() {
    Foo::staticDataMem = 5;   // set static data member
    Foo::staticMemFunc();     // call static member function
    // ...
}
```

The first line of `main()` sets the static data member; the second line invokes the static member function. (You may recall from the function invocation `ios::sync_with_stdio()` from Chapter 2, *C++ Without Classes*. You can now see that this is the invocation of a static member function of a class called `ios`.)

So we do not need to write `this->numElems`, we can just write `numElems`. The compiler knows we are referring to the `numElems` member of the `IntArray` instance for which this member function was called. Similarly, we can just write `elems` instead of `this->elems`.

Because almost every member function accesses other members of the same object, this is a convenient shorthand. From now on, we will write our member function definitions without `this`. As you will see in the next chapter, however, `this` still has its uses.

We can drop `this` inside member functions because a class creates its own scope. This scope falls in between the member function and the global scopes. In C, to find the declaration of an identifier used in a function, you simply examine each enclosing block, from the current to the global, until you find the declaration. In C++, to find the declaration of an identifier used in a member function, you examine the member function first as in C, then the class that the function is a member of, then the global scope. This intervening class scope is the structure OOP adds.

Figure 3-1 shows an example of the scopes in a C++ program. This particular program has two global functions and one class with three member functions. Some of the functions contain blocks inside them. Each scope can have identifiers declared in it and it can access the identifiers declared in an enclosing scope. For example, class data members live in the class scope and can be accessed by that class' member functions.

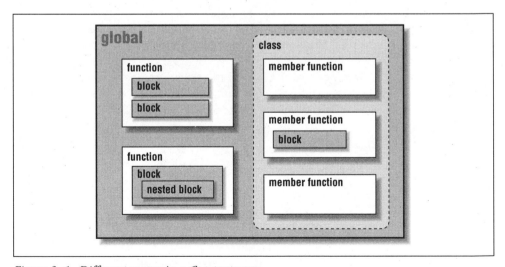

Figure 3-1: Different scopes in a C++ program

Of course, any time the compiler automates a task for us, like allowing us to drop `this`, we run the risk of confusing ourselves. Just as we have to worry about a local variable hiding a global with the same name in C, so now must we worry about locals shadowing class members and class members shadowing globals in C++.

Overloading Member Functions

Just like regular functions, member functions can be overloaded. One example of overloading is to use the same function name to get and set data in an object. Here's how we might get and set the number of elements in an IntArray:

```
class IntArray {
public:
    size_t size();              // instead of getSize()
    void size(size_t value);    // instead of setSize()
    // ...
};
```

When you call size(), the parameters you send it tell the compiler which function you mean.

4

Encapsulation with Access Specifiers

In the previous chapter we saw how classes support abstraction by providing member functions. Abstraction requires you to think carefully about your object's interface. After you've worked hard designing an interface, the last thing you want is for a user to go around it. So once you decide what the user *should* access, the next step in designing a class is to ensure this is all the user *can* access. In other words, you want to ensure the implementation details remain private. If you properly hide your implementation, you are free to change it as necessary without affecting other code. Keeping implementation details private is the realm of *encapsulation*, the focus of this chapter.

In C++, the class is the unit of encapsulation. The class is encapsulated through *access control*, that is, by controlling who has access to the class' members. As the programmer, you can declare which class members are accessible to users of the class and which are accessible only to the class itself. The members accessible outside the class create the interface to the class, that is, the capsule that encloses the implementation details.

Access Specifiers

Although we didn't discuss it, you have already seen one mechanism of access control in the previous chapter. It is handled by the public and private labels, which are called *access specifiers*. Here's a class definition with some public members and some private members:

```
// class with access specifiers
class IntArray {
public:    // this access specifier begins the class interface
    void init();
    void cleanup();
```

```
    void setSize(size_t value);
    size_t getSize();
    void setElem(size_t index, int value);
    int getElem(size_t index);

private:   // this access specifier begins the class implementation
    int *elems;
    size_t numElems;
};
```

Each access specifier determines which code can access the class members that follow it. The class members following a public label, called *public members*, can be accessed from any function, just like the fields of a struct. These create the class' interface. The class members following a private label, called *private members*, can only be accessed inside the class' own member functions (and by *friends*, which we'll introduce in the next section). Private members create the class' implementation.

Protected

There is also a third access specifier, protected. Protected members are like private members except they are accessible to *derived* classes. Derivation is discussed in Chapter 5, *Hierarchy with Composition and Derivation*.

To illustrate the effect of access specifiers, the following code contains *access violations*:

```
// function with access violations
main() {                   // not an IntArray member function
    IntArray nums;
    int *ptr;
    nums.init();           // ok: init() is a public member function
    nums.numElems = 5;     // access violation: numElems is a private data member
    ptr = nums.elems;      // access violation: elems is private data member
    nums.getSize();        // ok: getSize() is a public member function
}
```

Here the main() function cannot access private members of the IntArray class, numElems and elems, because it is not a member function of that class. The compiler catches these access violations, ensuring that code outside the class uses only the class' interface.

By contrast, every `IntArray` member function can access all members of that class, whether public or private:

```
// member function accessing private members
int IntArray::getElem(size_t index) {          // IntArray member function
    if (index >= numElems) error("bad index"); // ok to access numElems
    return elems[index];                       // ok to access elems
}
```

Here we see that `getElem()` can access the private `IntArray` members, `numElems` and `elems`. This function can access what `main()` above could not, because `getElem()` is a member of `IntArray`.

As we stated before, access control is enforced at the class level. This means that two different objects of the same class can access each others' private members. This allows us, for example, to create a member function that efficiently sets one object equal to another:

```
// IntArray member function accessing private members of two IntArray instances
void IntArray::assign(IntArray *source) {
    setSize(source->getSize());
    memcpy(elems, source->elems, getSize() * sizeof(int));
}
```

The object for which this member function is invoked copies the size and elements of the source object. On the second line of the function, the object accesses source's private data member `elems`. This code doesn't violate encapsulation because two instances of the same class share a common implementation.[*]

A Member Can Have Any Access Level

C++ allows any class member to have any *access level*. For example, even though we won't often show it, a class can have public data members. To illustrate, we could make the number of elements a public data member in our `IntArray` class:

```
// class with a public data member
class IntArray {
public:
    // ...
    size_t numElems;    // public data member: not recommended

private:
    int *elems;
};
```

---

[*] Some languages enforce access control at the object level—that is, no object has access to another's private members—but not C++.

struct Versus class

Up to now we've implied that structs in C++ are just like structs in C. In truth, structs in C++ have all the abilities of classes. They can have member functions, access specifiers, and everything else you'll learn classes can have. In fact, the only difference between structs and classes in C++ is that, for safety, the default access level of a class is private, while, for backwards compatibility, the default access level of a struct is public. A useful convention is to use structs like you did in C—as *plain old data structures*, with no member functions, access specifiers, or other fancy constructs—and classes as the basis of objects. Most C++ programmers follow this convention, but the language doesn't require it.

We might do this because we figure any implementation of `IntArray` will have a `numElems` member. Still, public data members expose the class implementation, so use them with care.

Private member functions, on the other hand, are common and often useful. For example, because more than one `IntArray` member function needs range checking, we might create a function to perform this task:

```
// class with a private member function
class IntArray {
    // ...
private:
    void checkIndex(size_t index); // private member func: often useful
    // ...
};
```

The `checkIndex()` function is not meant to be part of the class interface, so we make it private. Access to this private member function is restricted just like for private data members. Any `IntArray` member function can access a private member function:

```
// calling a private member function from within the class
int IntArray::getElem(size_t index) { // IntArray member function
    checkIndex(index);                 // ok: private member of same class
    return elems[index];
}
```

And a function that is not an `IntArray` member cannot access private member functions:

```
    // calling a private member function from outside the class (illegal)
    void SomeClass::someMemFunc() {        // not an IntArray member function
        IntArray nums;
        nums.checkIndex(5);                // access violation
    }
```

Unlimited Access Specifiers

C++ puts no restrictions on the order or number of access specifiers in a class. The following is perfectly valid:

```
    class Foo {              // order and number of access specifiers not restricted
        int privData1;       // private by default, not recommended
        void privFunc1();
    public:
        int pubData;
        void pubFunc1();
    private:
        void privFunc2();
    private:
        double privData2;
    public:
        void pubFunc3();
    };
```

The first two members are private by default. This default acts as a security measure by requiring that you explicitly grant public access to a member. Keep this in mind, because you will sometimes forget to put access specifiers in a class declaration and therefore receive compilation errors when you try to use the class' interface. To avoid confusion, it's a good idea to explicitly specify the access level of all members. All members listed after an access specifier have the same access level, until the next access specifier.

Private Does Not Mean Invisible

In C, the only form of encapsulation is invisibility. That is, the only way to prevent unauthorized access to functions or data is to use the static keyword to hide them in their own code file. In C++, encapsulation is enforced by controlling access, not visibility.[*] The class user can see all class members, public and private, in the header file. It is access control, not visibility control, that prevents unauthorized use of class members. This has two implications which we discuss now.

---

[*] You are free, of course, to use the C encapsulation method as well. We can even bless it by calling it a distinct access level, the *implementation level*. It is usually not worth the effort to use in C++, however.

Encapsulation Protects Against Accident, Not Malice

Encapsulation in C++ is really a protection against accident, not malice. It prevents you from mistakenly calling a private member function, but it does not prevent you from using a cast to subvert the type system and write on private data members. Nor does it prevent you from examining the private members of a class declaration and making assumptions about the implementation. In the spirit of C, C++ assumes that as long as it protects you from accidental violations, the purposeful ones are your own concern.

Overloading Resolution Ignores Access Level

A class member's access level only affects which code can access it. It is not part of a member function's signature and is not repeated when the member function is defined. This means that access considerations do not influence which overloaded function the compiler chooses. So, given the class:

```
class Foo {
public:
    func(int intParam);
private:
    func(char charParam);
};
```

the following code results in an access violation:

```
main() {
    Foo someFoo;
    someFoo.func('a');     // access violation: resolves to Foo::func(char)
}                          // even though it's a private member function
```

You may think that this code will convert `'a'` to an `int` and call `Foo::func(int)` because doing so is the only legal option. The compiler, however, resolves calls to member functions without regard to access level. Only *after* the compiler has resolved function calls does it check the access level of the function and complain if there is a violation. This method results in fewer surprises if you change a member function's access level. Just remember that the compiler chooses the matching function, even if it is illegal, and then complains if necessary.

Friend Classes

Up to this point, we have assumed that an abstraction can be captured as a single class. The access control mechanisms shown so far work nicely in this case. You just make the interface public and the implementation private in the same class and all the interface functions can access the implementation. Access control can get in the way, however, when an abstraction requires two or more classes to work closely together. This section tells how cooperating classes share private information without allowing other classes to violate the combined abstraction.

An Example of Cooperating Classes

To see how two or more classes can work together to create a single abstraction, consider containers. Containers come in an endless variety: from humble arrays to not-so-humble b-trees and beyond. Their variety and utility make them a staple of programming courses and C++ books. Here is a stack implemented using our IntArray class:

```
// a stack class
class IntStack {
public:
    void init();
    void cleanup();
    void push(int value);    // add new top item
    void pop();              // remove top item
    int peek();              // return top item
    int isEmpty();           // is there a top item

private:
    IntArray items;          // storage for stack items
    size_t depth;            // number of items on stack
};
```

This IntStack has the standard housekeeping functions init() and cleanup() and the standard stack functions push() and pop(). The stack user can also peek() at the top element without popping it off and call isEmpty() to check if anything is on the stack. The stack elements are stored in items, with depth telling how many elements are in the stack so far.

Sometimes you want to perform an operation on all the elements of a container, like printing each one. Such operations require the ability to iterate over all the elements. In the case of a stack we could require the user to pop all the elements off, one at a time. A better solution is to add extra member functions to the container class to return each successive element. Our stack then looks like this:

```
// stack class with members that support iteration
class IntStack {
public:
    // ...keep all the member functions we showed above and add these new ones:
    void goFirst();      // reset iteration pointer to first item
    void goNext();       // move iteration pointer to next item
    int getCur();        // get current item
    int curIsValid();    // is the current item valid

private:
```

```
    // ...keep all the data we showed above and add this new piece:
    size_t curItem;      // index of current item
};
```

To our simple stack we have added a member function to iterate over the stack elements and return the current one. The new data member `curItem` keeps our place in the iteration.

A few problems result from this solution. First, it complicates the interface. Extra member functions to iterate through our `IntStack` (or any container class) make the class more complex. Second, we need extra data members, like `curItem`, to enable this iteration. The extra members entail a size increase for every object, even though some objects might not need iteration capabilities. Finally, the biggest problem is that we can have only one current iteration on a container. This restriction makes a simple task like checking a container for duplicate elements quite hard to implement.

Here's where the cooperating class comes in: the standard solution to these iteration problems is to place the iteration functionality in a separate class called an *iterator.*[*] Just like the member functions we added to `IntStack` above, an iterator class lets you traverse the members of a container, one element at a time. Unlike the member-function solution, a separate iterator class only takes up space if you use it and it lets you create as many active iterators on a container as you like. We now declare an iterator for our `IntStack` class, calling it `IntStackIter`. The function names are the same, but now they're gone from the `IntStack` class and placed in the `IntStackIter` class:

```
    // a class that iterates over an IntStack
    class IntStackIter {
    public:
        // housekeeping
        void init();
        void cleanup();

        // set stack to iterate over
        void setIter(IntStack *stack);

        // these the same as in the previous solution
        void goFirst();
        void goNext();
        int getCur();
        int curIsValid();

    private:
        IntStack *iterStack;    // stack to iterate over
        size_t curItem;         // index of current item in stack
    };
```

----

* It is also called a *cursor* or *scanner.*

You've seen most of these class members before. The new member function `setIter()` allows you to tell the `IntStackIter` which `IntStack` to iterate over. This is stored in the data member `iterStack`.

As you might suspect, the implementation of an iterator is closely tied to the implementation of the container it iterates over. In addition to storing the stack to iterate over in `iterStack`, for example, an `IntStackIter` object stores the index of the current stack element in the iteration. If we implemented `IntStack` with a linked list, the iterator would contain a pointer to the current element instead of a count. In other words, the iterator needs access not just to the stack's interface, but also to its implementation.

Now that we've defined the iterator, we can use it to sum the elements on the stack:

```
// using a stack iterator
main() {
    IntStack stack;
    IntStackIter iter;
    int sum;
    // ...
    stack.init();
    iter.init();
    // ...
    sum = 0;
    iter.setIter(&stack);
    for (iter.goFirst(); iter.curIsValid(); iter.goNext())
        sum += iter.getCur();
    // ...
    iter.cleanup();
    stack.cleanup();
}
```

The interesting code is in the `for` loop, where we use `iter` to access the elements of stack and compute their sum. We have now created two classes that need to work closely together. The next section shows how we prevent access control from getting in the way of this cooperation.

Giving a Class Special Access

As we said, to do its job, an iterator needs access to the innards of the container over which it iterates. For example, the `getCur()` member function could be implemented as follows:

```
int IntStackIter::getCur() {
    if (!curIsValid()) error("no current item");
    return iterStack->items.getElem(curItem);
}
```

This shows an `IntStackIter` member function accessing `items`, a private data member of `IntStack`. As we know, a class usually cannot access another class' private members like this. To allow it, `IntStack` declares `IntStackIter` to be a *friend*:

```
class IntStack {
    friend class IntStackIter;      // friend declaration

public:
    // everything else is unchanged...
};
```

This friend declaration says that `IntStackIter` has access to all of `IntStack`. In other words, `IntStackIter` member functions can access the private members of `IntStack`. So the definition of `getCur()` above will not cause an access violation. `IntStackIter` is called a *friend class* of `IntStack`.*

Friend Functions

A class can make an individual function a friend. This function then has access to the class' private members without itself being a member of that class. Here is an example:

```
class SomeClass {
    friend void someFunc();      // friend function declaration
    // ...
};
void someFunc() {/*...*/}
```

The function `someFunc()` is not a member of class `SomeClass`. The friend declaration in `SomeClass`, however, grants the function access to `SomeClass` as if it were a member function.

The keyword `class` is not needed in the friend declaration if the friend class has already been declared. Because friend classes depend on the class that grants friendship, however, they are usually declared after that class.

Friend declarations can go anywhere in the class. Access specifiers do not affect friend declarations. Usually, programmers put friend declarations first, before the class members. This convention immediately alerts readers to other important classes.

---

* This is where most texts point out that C++ is the language that allows your friends to access your private parts. We refrain from making such observations.

Note that one class *grants* friendship to another. The above declaration does not give `IntStack` any special access to the innards of `IntStackIter`; if it did, one class could easily violate another's encapsulation by declaring itself a friend.[*]

Now suppose that `IntStack`'s friend `IntStackIter` makes yet another class, `Iter-Friend`, a friend:

```
class IntStackIter {
    friend class IterFriend;
    // ...
};
```

Even though `IterFriend` is a friend of `IntStackIter` which is a friend of `IntStack`, `IterFriend` is *not* a friend of `IntStack`. This is usually stated, "my friend's friend is not automatically my friend" or, more formally, "friendship is not transitive."

Friendship allows classes to work together by granting a specific class increased access to another. Like casts, or any feature that lets you suspend a language's normal security, friendship can be misused. Redesigning your abstractions might be a better solution at times. Use friendship to create a unified interface out of more than one class, never as a work-around for improperly designed abstractions.

---

[*] A discussion of whether *friend* is a good word to describe a relationship that is not symmetric will be deferred until our next book, a penetrating study, *This Friend Has Class: A Psychological Profile of C++ Programmers Based on Their Code.*

5

Hierarchy with Composition and Derivation

One of the benefits of proper abstraction is code reuse. We can create new abstractions using ones we've already implemented and tested, incrementally building complex systems. Object-oriented languages provide two mechanisms for building these hierarchies: composition and derivation. We cover them both in this chapter, but most of the chapter is devoted to derivation because composition is used in C, while derivation is not.

Composition

So far we've taken data members for granted because their use mimics that of struct fields. When we design the interface to a class, data members play a secondary role to member functions. The correct data members, however, can make implementing a class much easier. In the previous chapter, we implemented IntStack using our IntArray, like this:

```
class IntStack {      // an IntStack is composed from...
    // ...
private:
    IntArray items; // an IntArray
    size_t depth;   // and a size_t
};
```

Creating objects with other objects as members is called *composition.*[*] The example above uses IntArray instead of C's built-in array, allowing us to avoid repeating work like range checking. Using IntArray rather than a linked-list class that we haven't created yet allows us to quickly get our IntStack going. Once we have our classes working together, we can optimize for size, speed, or flexibility as needed.

---

[*] Alternatively *aggregation* or *layering*.

Compose your classes using the most powerful tools at hand, especially when you are just beginning to understand the language.

Derivation

Derivation allows a class to not only use another class for its implementation, but also to share that class' interface. For example, we might want to expand the IntArray class so it can sort itself. If we decide that we want this sortable array to be a new class, we will certainly base it on our existing IntArray class. If we use composition, it would look like this:

```
class SortIntArray {    // composed from IntArray
public:
    void sort();        // new member function
    void setSize();     // interface from IntArray
    int getSize();
    // ...

private:
    IntArray array;     // this IntArray does most of the real work
    int *sortBuf;       // we might need this to help us sort
};
```

The first member function, sort(), is new. The other ones are just repeated from IntArray; each will simply call the appropriate member function on the array data member that does the real work. Of course, if IntArray's interface is ever changed, we need to make appropriate changes in SortIntArray.

This repetitive and burdensome labor is avoided with derivation. The following example shows functionally equivalent code using derivation:

```
class SortIntArray : public IntArray { // derived from IntArray
public:
    void sort();
private:
    int *sortBuf;
};
```

Note that setSize(), getSize(), and the other functions from IntArray are not repeated in SortIntArray. The : public IntArray says that SortIntArray is derived from IntArray. This means it is an extension of that class. More specifically, it means an instance of IntArray is embedded in SortIntArray and all IntArray's public members are accessible through instances of SortIntArray. We say that SortIntArray *inherits* functionality from IntArray. Here is a sample of usage:

```
main() {
    SortIntArray howDoILoveThee;
    // ...
```

```
        howDoILoveThee.setSize(WAYS_COUNT);     // inherited from IntArray
        // ...
        howDoILoveThee.sort();                  // new to SortIntArray
        // ...
    }
```

Here we see that, even though we didn't give `SortIntArray` a `setSize()` member function, we can call this member function on an instance of this class. All of `IntArray`'s public members can be accessed like this. `IntArray` is called the *base class*. `SortIntArray` is called the *derived class*. Figure 5-1 shows how we typically draw this relationship, in a *derivation tree*. The arrow points from the derived class to the base class to show that the derived class uses the base class.[*]

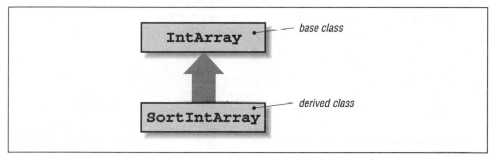

Figure 5–1: Two classes related by derivation

A class can be a base class of any number of other classes. A derived class can also be a base class for further derived classes. We might decide that we want our sortable array to make us coffee:

```
class SortIntArrayThatMakesCoffee : public SortIntArray {
public:
    void howManyCups(int num);
    void makeCoffee();
private:
    int numberOfCups;
};
```

This inherits all of `SortIntArray`'s public members. This includes the `IntArray`'s public members. Figure 5-2 shows the relationship between these three classes.

So you can derive from a class whether or not it's derived from another class. But you cannot derive from built-in types:

```
class MyInt : public int {/*...*/};     // not allowed in C++
```

---

* Other languages call the base class the *superclass* and the derived class the *subclass*. The prefixes refer to the position of the class in a derivation tree.

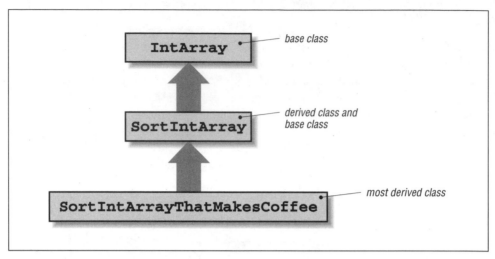

Figure 5–2: Three classes related by derivation

In the example above we are trying to create a class that has all the functionality of an int, with some added functionality of our own. We can't do it because int is a built-in type. We must use composition instead.

In the next four sections we discuss implications of derivation on concepts we've covered previously. These sections cover:

Encapsulation
    Does derivation reduce the protection afforded by encapsulation?

Pointer conversion
    What is the relationship between a pointer to a base class and a pointer to its derived class?

Member-function overloading
    What happens when you overload a base class function in a derived class?

Member-function overriding
    What if you want to change the behavior of a base-class function in a derived class?

Encapsulation and Derivation

Derivation allows you to use an existing class as the basis for a new class. It's the closest sharing you can have without adding directly to the original class. Altering a class—say to add your own sort() to someone else's IntArray class—would be a violation of encapsulation. The power of derivation is that it is a close form of sharing that maintains encapsulation between the two classes.

One implication of this is that the derived class cannot access the base class' private members, as `Derived` tries to do here:

```
class Base {
public:
    void pubB();
private:
    void privB();
};

class Derived : public Base {
public:
    void pubD();
private:
    void privD();
};

void Derived::pubD() {
    privD();    // ok: private member of Derived
    pubB();     // ok: public member of Base
    privB();    // access violation: private member of Base
}
```

Class `Derived` is derived from class `Base`. The `Derived` member function `pubD()` can access the private `Derived` member `privD()` and the public `Base` member `pubB()`. This function cannot access the private `Base` member `privB()`, however.

`Derived` access to private members of base classes can be a confusing point, because you are encouraged to think of derivation as allowing you to extend classes. In a sense this is true. It is true that the base class' public members seem like they are part of the derived class. But `Base`'s private members are still not accessible to `Derived`. So derivation provides a controlled way to extend one class into another.

Another example of encapsulation not being violated is that friendship and derivation are completely separate. Consider the hierarchy shown in Figure 5-3, in which B1 has granted friendship to B2, and D1 and D2 are derived from B1 and B2.

B2 has special access to B1 because B1 gives it that access by declaring it a friend. As a result, you might expect B2 to also have special access to a class derived from B1, like D1. Alternatively, you might expect a class derived from B2—like D2—to have special access to B1. In both cases, you'd be wrong. Friendship does not survive derivation. To use more informal language: your friend's child isn't necessarily your friend and your friend isn't necessarily your child's friend. No class is a friend of any other unless friendship is explicitly granted in the class definition.

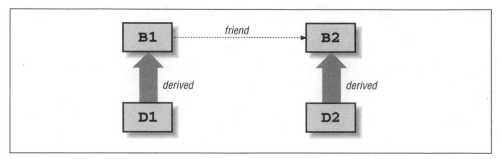

Figure 5–3: Four classes related by derivation and friendship

Automatic Pointer Conversion

Because the derived class contains a superset of the base class functionality, C++ allows us to treat a derived-class instance as a base-class instance, when we want to. You might, for example, have a function that averages an `IntArray`:

```
int average(IntArray *ia) {/*calculate average*/}
```

We can pass it an instance of a class derived from `IntArray`, like `SortIntArray`:

```
main() {
    SortIntArray sia;
    // ...
    i = average(&sia); // passing a SortIntArray* where IntArray* is expected
    // ...               // the compiler allows this without a cast
}
```

Here we pass a pointer to a `SortIntArray` to a function that expects a pointer to its base class, `IntArray`. The compiler automatically converts a derived-class pointer to a base-class pointer without complaint. Note that this is a truly type-safe conversion because the derived object can do what the base object can. The compiler guarantees that, inside `average()`, ia points to the `IntArray` part of the `SortIntArray` instance sia.[*]

The reverse cast, from a base-class pointer to a derived-class pointer, cannot be done implicitly. In other words, you cannot pass an `IntArray` to a function that expects a `SortIntArray`. This is not safe because the derived class can do things that the base class cannot. Here are some conversions to illustrate what is and is not allowed:

---

[*] The actual value of the pointer does not need to change during the conversion, though it may, depending on compiler. The base class can be stored at the beginning of the derived class in memory, in which case one pointer actually points to both of them.

Private Derivation

What we've been calling derivation in this chapter is actually *public* derivation. Remember the unexplained public keyword in the declaration of a derived class:

```
class SortIntArray : public IntArray {/*...*/};
                   // ^^^^^^ we now explain what
                   // "public" means here
```

This keyword tells you the level of access to the base class allowed to users of the derived class. Because IntArray is a *public* base class, SortIntArray users can access the IntArray part of SortIntArray instances. This is why we can access IntArray's interface through SortIntArray instances and why we can convert a SortIntArray pointer to an IntArray pointer without a cast.

If we made IntArray a *private* base class, like this:

```
class SortIntArray : private IntArray {/*...*/};
                   // ^^^^^^^ IntArray is a private base class
```

a SortIntArray user could not access the IntArray part of SortIntArray objects. In other words, IntArray's interface would not be part of SortIntArray's and we could not freely convert derived-class pointers to base-class pointers.

The uses of private derivation is an advanced topic. We mention it only to explain the public keyword. Also, private derivation is the default, so don't forget the public keyword. Having to specify public is a slight nuisance, but it is consistent with the idea that access should be restricted by default.

```
main() {
    IntArray ia, *pia;          // base-class object and pointer
    SortIntArray sia, *psia;    // derived-class object and pointer

    pia = &sia;                 // safe: derived- to base-class pointer
    psia = pia;                 // unsafe and not allowed: base- to derived-
                                //     class pointer needs a cast
    psia = (SortIntArray *)pia; // unsafe but allowed: ok because object is
                                //     really a SortIntArray
    psia = (SortIntArray *)&ia; // unsafe but allowed: error because object is
                                //     not a SortIntArray
}
```

First, we point pia, an IntArray pointer, at sia, a SortIntArray instance. The compiler allows this, making sure that pia points to the IntArray part of sia. Next, we try to point psia, a SortIntArray pointer, at what the IntArray pointer pia points to. This is unsafe and requires a cast to tell the compiler to allow it. We add this cast in the third assignment, which is like the second assignment, but with a cast telling the compiler to ignore the type violation. As it turns out, because the first assignment made pia point to a SortIntArray instance, the cast will not get you in trouble.

In the final assignment, we use a cast to prevent the compiler from complaining when we point the SortIntArray pointer psia at ia, an IntArray instance. The cast keeps the compiler quiet, but this assignment is surely trouble. If we try to access data members existing only in SortIntArray, for example, we'll be accessing data that is not part of ia.

Casting from a derived- to a base-class pointer is called *up-casting*. Casting from a base- to a derived-class pointer is called *down-casting*. The prefixes refer to the direction of travel in the derivation tree. They are also the direction the corners of your mouth should go when you think about doing each kind of cast.

Multiple Inheritance

A class can have more than one base class. You might define a piece of hypertext as:

```
class HyperText : public EventClass, public GraphicsClass {/*...*/};
```

where EventClass handles the events and GraphicsClass handles the drawing. This simple change from *single* to *multiple* inheritance actually introduces a number of subtle problems that make multiple inheritance an advanced feature.

One problem is name clashes. If EventClass and GraphicsClass both coincidentally contain a check() member function, which one does the HyperText class inherit? It inherits both, but you must ensure that a call to this function is unambiguous. Another problem is multiple inclusion of a base class. If EventClass and GraphicsClass are both derived from MyClass, does HyperText contain one or two copies of that class? It turns out that it contains two copies, unless you make MyClass a *virtual* base class.

Dangerous Array Conversion

A pointer to an array of derived-class objects should not be converted to a base-class pointer. This example shows how array conversions can get us in trouble:

```
main() {
    Derived d[5];      // array of Derived objects
    Base *b = d;       // danger: shouldn't do this
    b++;               // this is the problem
    b->alter();        // sorrow: almost certain bit munching
}
```

The compiler allows the pointer conversion. It can't, in general, know whether a pointer is pointing to an object or an array of objects. The problem is that when the Base pointer b is incremented, the address is changed based on the size of Base. Base is usually not the same size as Derived. So the pointer ends up between objects. This is another reason to use an array class instead of the built-in array.

Member Function Overloading

As described in Chapter 3, *Abstraction with Member Functions*, when you have many functions with the same name in a single class, the compiler chooses the best match for any given use. Here we have a class with two func() member functions:

```
class Base {
  public:
    void func(int i);      // two overloaded member functions
    void func(char c);
};

main() {
    Base b;
    b.func(5);             // invokes Base::func(int)
    b.func('5');           // invokes Base::func(char)
}
```

If you add a function with the same name in a derived class, however, this function doesn't, as you might expect, become just another function the compiler can choose. Instead, this new derived-class function hides all the functions in the base class with the same name, much like a local variable hides a global with the same name. Here we derive a class from Base and add another func() member function:

```
class Derived : public Base {
public:
    void func(double d); // has the same name as two Base member functions
};

main() {
    Derived d;
```

```
    d.func('x');          // surprise: invokes Derived::func(double)
}                         //              not Base::func(char)
```

We might be trying to call `Base::func(char)`, but it is hidden by `Derived::func(double)`. It's possible to find even sillier situations:

```
class Derived2 : public Base {
public:
    void func();  // has the same name as two Base member functions
};

main() {
    Derived2 d2;
    d2.func('x'); // surprise: compilation error
}
```

Here you obviously want `Base::func(char)`. The compiler, however, resolves to `Derived2::func()` and then says you have a parameter mismatch.

This perhaps nonintuitive resolution rule is used to prevent surprises if a new function is added to a base class. For example, if base-class functions could overload derived-class functions and we add a `Base::func(float)` function at some later time, a user of `Derived` might find that calls that were going to `Derived::func(double)` are now going to our new function. This was considered dangerous and confusing. So derived-class functions hide, rather than overload, base-class functions of the same name.[*]

It is unlikely you'll be designing derivation hierarchies in which you want multi-level function overloading. If you do, you can still access the hidden base-class member functions. You need to *qualify* the function name:

```
main() {
    Derived d;
    d.Base::func('x');    // ok: qualified name
}
```

Putting the class before the function tells the compiler to begin resolution with the class `Base`.

Member Function Overriding

Sometimes you want to change the behavior of a base-class function in a derived class. For example, say you have a `Fraction` class that represents a fractional number:

---

[*] Recall that as we said in Chapter 3, a class creates its own scope. You can consider the derived class' scope to be nested inside the base class' scope. Viewed in this way, the resolution rules (derived names hiding base names) make more sense.

```
class Fraction {                          // stores a fraction
public:
    void set(int numer, int denom); // set fraction to some value
    int getNumer();                       // returns numerator
    int getDenom();                       // returns denominator

private:
    int numerator;                        // top of fraction
    int denominator;                      // bottom of fraction
};
```

This class stores and returns the numerator and denominator of a fraction. Now say you want a class `Rational` that represents a fraction, but is always in lowest terms (e.g., ½ rather than ¾). If you derive it from `Fraction`, you'll want to change `set()` to keep the fraction in lowest terms. You might try simply redeclaring `set()`:

```
class Rational : public Fraction {  // a rational is a fraction in lowest terms
public:
    void set(int numer, int denom); // redeclaration of set()
};
```

The declaration of `Rational::set()` is identical to the one in `Fraction::set()`. This allows you to supply a new definition that overrides the version in `Fraction`.

Unfortunately, there are times when the compiler invokes the wrong version of `set()`, possibly leaving a `Rational` instance in the wrong form. Overriding base-class functions to change their behavior is part of polymorphism, and we cover this in Chapter 12, *Polymorphism with Virtual Functions*. For now, do not override base-class functions. To implement `Rational` without polymorphism, you must use composition instead of derivation, that is, make `Rational` have a data member of type `Fraction`. The part of `Rational`'s interface that is identical to `Fraction`'s can call the appropriate member function on the `Fraction` data member.

The only exception to the "don't override base-class functions" rule involves basic functions that almost every class needs. Most classes need to initialize themselves before they are used. We've supplied an `init()` function for this purpose. A derived class needs its own version of this function, so you may override it in this case. We discuss this further in the next section.

Chaining

Often, the major work of a class' member function is handled by calling similar member functions in each of that class' members. For example, a function like init() must initialize the base-class part and all the data members of a derived class instance. Here's an example using SortIntArray, which derives from IntArray:

```
class SortIntArray : public IntArray {
public:
    void init();
    // ...
private:
    SomeClass someData;
    int *sortBuf;
};

void SortIntArray::init() {
    // chaining
    IntArray::init();      // chain to base class init()
    someData.init();       // chain to data member init()
    sortBuf = 0;           // chain to built-in type's assignment

    // other stuff
    cout << "SortIntArray initialized\n";
}
```

Here we see a member function calling similar member functions for each class member. This is called *chaining up the class hierarchy* or, simply, *chaining*. First, we initialize the base class. We need to use the qualified name IntArray::init() to avoid invoking SortIntArray::init() recursively. Then we initialize the data members. We call init() on a data member that is a class. Because built-in types have no init(), we chain to the assignment operator. This is still considered chaining because the assignment operator is as close as a built-in type has to an init() function.

You might think that chaining is so obvious in this case that the compiler should handle it for you. In fact, the compiler does such *automatic* chaining for some member functions. We discuss this in the next chapter.

6

Better Abstraction with Constructors and Destructors

Now that you've seen the basics of abstraction, encapsulation, and hierarchy in C++, you are ready to learn more advanced features. One of the goals of C++ is to make class instances as easy to use as instances of built-in types. This is an advanced form of abstraction: abstracting away whether a type is built-in or user-defined. C++ provides special member functions to help with this kind of abstraction. You learn about two of them in this chapter.

Each class we created in the previous chapters had an init() and a cleanup() member function to handle initialization and clean up of objects. C++ provides special member functions, called *constructors* and *destructors*, to ensure that these tasks are performed at the correct times.

The Default Constructor

A constructor is a special member function that initializes a class instance. A class can have any number of constructors, distinguished by the parameters they take. Each constructor can initialize a class instance differently. In this section we introduce the most important constructor, called the *default constructor*. We discuss other constructors in Chapter 9, *Better Abstraction with Other Special Member Functions*.

Definition of Default Constructor

A constructor has the same name as the class it constructs.[*] Instead of the `init()` function our `IntArray` class had in previous chapters, it now has a default constructor:

```
class IntArray {
public:
    IntArray();           // default constructor declaration:
    // ...                 // named after class, no return type
private:
    int *elems;
    size_t numElems;
};

IntArray::IntArray() {    // default constructor definition:
    numElems = 0;         // does what init() did
    elems = 0;
}
```

A constructor has no return type, not even `void`. The default constructor takes no parameters. Its definition may look odd, beginning with `IntArray::IntArray`. Remember that the first `IntArray` determines the class of which the function is a member. The second `IntArray` is the name of the function.

A common mistake is to use this qualified name `IntArray::IntArray` on the declaration as well:

```
class IntArray {
public:
    IntArray::IntArray(); // wrong: don't qualify name in declaration
    IntArray();           // right: unqualified name in declaration
    // ...
};
```

The `IntArray::` prefix is unnecessary and illegal here—as it would be on any member function—because the declaration is lexically inside the class.

Invocation of Default Constructor

Now that we've put the `IntArray` initialization code into the default constructor, the compiler ensures that the code is invoked when necessary. For example, the declaration of an `IntArray` object—like `nums` below—causes a call to the `IntArray` default constructor:

---

[*] This is not quite true for class templates. See Chapter 11, *Better Hierarchy with Templates*, for the details.

```
main() {
    IntArray nums;        // this declaration causes a default constructor call
                          // note nums.init() call seen in previous chapters
                          // not needed anymore
    nums.setSize(5);
    // ...
}
```

Instead of needing an explicit call to init(), nums is initialized by an automatic invocation of the default constructor. We say that nums is *default constructed*.

The class user's code is now shorter and safer. The compiler ensures that the object is initialized. This automatic initialization becomes increasingly useful as you build complex objects, saving you typing and debugging time.

Side Effects in Constructor

A constructor can contain any code other member functions can. For instance, we can add a side effect, like a print statement, to a constructor to see exactly when it is invoked:

```
IntArray::IntArray() {     // default constructor with side effect
    cout << "in IntArray default constructor, object address "
        << this << '\n';
    // ...
}
```

This default constructor prints a message telling the class and the address of the object being constructed. If we run the following program:

```
main() {
    IntArray int_o_rama;
    IntArray int_fest;
    cout << "IntArrays declared, object address "
        << &int_o_rama << " and " << &int_fest << '\n';
}
```

on one of our machines, it produces:

```
in IntArray default constructor, object address 0xbffffe38
in IntArray default constructor, object address 0xbffffe34
IntArrays declared, object address 0xbffffe38 and 0xbffffe34
```

The construction of int_o_rama and int_fest prints the first two lines. The last statement of main() prints the third line.

The Destructor

A destructor is the constructor's counterpart for controlling the lifetime of an object. It cleans up the object when you no longer need it, freeing the resources it holds.

Definition of Destructor

A destructor is named after the class it destroys, preceded by a tilde.[*] Its name is an attempt to convey that it *complements* the constructor. Instead of the cleanup() function our class had in previous chapters, it now has a destructor:

```
class IntArray {
public:
    IntArray();         // default constructor declaration
    ~IntArray();        // destructor declaration: named after class
    // ...               //                         no return type
private:
    int *elems;
    size_t numElems;
};

IntArray::~IntArray() { // destructor definition: does what cleanup() did
    if (elems != 0) free(elems);
}
```

Each class has a single destructor. It takes no parameters and has no return type. Like a constructor, a destructor can contain any code you want.

Invocation of Destructor

The compiler ensures that the destructor is invoked when the object can no longer be used. For example, an automatic local object—like a1 and a2 below—is destroyed when the flow of control leaves its enclosing block:

```
main() {
    IntArray a1;     // a1 constructed here
    if (something) {
        IntArray a2; // a2 constructed here
        // ...
    }                // a2 destroyed here
}                    // a1 destroyed here
```

Here a1's destructor is invoked when main() returns. Before this, a2 is destroyed when the flow of control leaves the if statement.

---

* Again, see Chapter 11, for the truth about class templates.

Built-in Types

Instances of built-in types are still not automatically initialized by C++. So, you must initialize built-in types explicitly, as you do in C:

```
main() {
    int a;              // a is in an unknown state, must assign to it later
    char *b = 0;        // b is explicitly put into a known state
    IntArray c;         // c is automatically put into a known state, assuming
    // ...               //     default constructor is defined correctly
}
```

In this example, a is in an unknown state because it is an instance of a built-in type and is not explicitly initialized like b. Because c is a class instance, its default constructor is automatically invoked, putting it into a known state.

Instances of built-in types are also not automatically destroyed. This is only a problem for pointer instances, because other types have no resources you need to free. Lack of automatic construction and destruction is one of the ways built-in types and classes differ.

Hierarchy and Chaining

At the end of Chapter 5, *Hierarchy with Composition and Derivation*, we said many member functions chain, that is, call similar member functions on the class' members. We showed that a class' init() member function, for instance, must call init() for the base class and data members of that class. With constructors and destructors, the work of chaining is done for you. In this section we explore this automatic chaining.

A Class Hierarchy

To demonstrate automatic chaining, let's create a simple class hierarchy in which a TextBox is derived from a simple Rect and composed of a Color, an int, and a char*:

```
class Rect {            // simple rectangle
public:
    Rect();
    ~Rect();
    // ...              // ignore rest of interface so we can focus on hierarchy
private:
    int left, top;      // upper-left corner
    int width, height;  // size
};

class Color {     // graphics color
public:
```

```
        Color();
        ~Color();
        // ...
    private:
        int data;      // color is stored compactly in an integer
    };

    class TextBox : public Rect { // a text box is a rectangle plus...
    public:
        TextBox();
        ~TextBox();
        // ...
    private:
        Color textColor;          // color to draw text in
        int frameThickness;       // thickness of boundary in pixels
        char *text;               // text to draw
    };
```

This hierarchy has a typical mix of classes and built-in types related by composition and derivation. It is drawn in Figure 6-1.

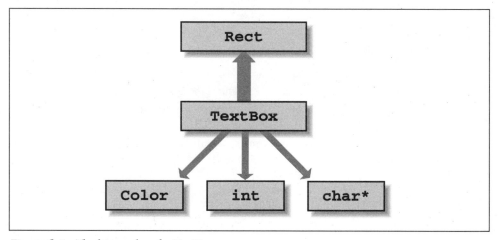

Figure 6-1: The hierarchy of a TextBox

We have created this hierarchy to show what the constructors and destructors look like. Here they are for `Rect`:

```
Rect::Rect() {
    left = top = width = height = 0;
    cout << "in default constructor for: Rect\n";
}

Rect::~Rect() {cout << "in destructor for: Rect\n";}
```

Rect's default constructor must put its members into a known state because they are all ints and do not default construct themselves. It then prints out a message so we know it has run. This will help us below. Any additional work that the default constructor needs to do would go where this print statement is, after the data members have been assigned. The destructor has no work to do. It just prints out some text.

The default constructor and destructor for Color is much the same. Things get interesting with TextBox:

```
TextBox::TextBox() {
    frameThickness = 0;
    text = 0;
    cout << "in default constructor for: TextBox\n";
}

// assume a member function that sets text with malloc()

TextBox::~TextBox() {
    cout << "in destructor for: TextBox\n";
    if (text != 0) free(text);
}
```

TextBox's default constructor explicitly assigns only to the data members that are instances of built-in types, that is, frameThickness and text. Its Rect base class and textColor data member certainly need to have their default constructors called, but this is done automatically. A class' default constructor automatically chains to the default constructors of its base class and members that are instances of classes. When the body of the default constructor is entered, these members have already been constructed. So the TextBox default constructor must only assign to its members that are instances of built-in types.

The TextBox destructor has only one real task: free the malloc()ed memory pointed to by text. The frameThickness data member has no resources to free because it is an int. The destructors for the Rect base class and textColor data member are automatically chained to. They are invoked *after* the class' destructor exits. This way you may access these class members inside the destructor body.

If we run this program:

```
main() {
    TextBox tbox;      // instantiate TextBox
    cout << "-->main() complete<--\n";
}
```

we get this output:

```
in default constructor for: Rect
in default constructor for: Color
in default constructor for: TextBox
-->main() complete<--
in destructor for: TextBox
```

```
in destructor for: Color
in destructor for: Rect
```

Inside `main()` we first declare tbox, a `TextBox` instance. This declaration invokes the `TextBox` default constructor. Then `main()` prints a message. Finally, when `main()` exits, tbox's destructor is invoked.

The messages show us the order of construction and destruction of the `TextBox` object. Notice how the `Rect` and then the `Color` default constructor are invoked before the `TextBox` default constructor. On the other hand, the `TextBox` destructor is completed before the `Color` and then the `Rect` destructors are called.

This order is important because it guarantees that, inside the `TextBox` constructor and destructor, its members are in a known state. A class' base class is constructed first, then its data members are constructed, and finally its own constructor is called. Destruction happens in the reverse order.

Arrays

Before we leave the subject of construction and destruction, we turn our attention to arrays. When an array of objects is created, the default constructor is called on each element. The objects are constructed in order of increasing address, that is, increasing index, starting with the rightmost index in a multidimensional array:

```
Rect r1[3];     // construction order: r1[0], r1[1], r1[2]
Rect r2[3][3]; // construction order: r2[0][0], r2[0][1], ..., r2[2][2]
```

The elements are destroyed in reverse order when the array is destroyed. If we run this program:

```
main() {
    TextBox tbox[2];     // instantiate array of two TextBoxes
    printf("-->main() complete<--\n");
}
```

we get this output:

```
in default constructor for: Rect        <-- for tbox[0]
in default constructor for: Color
in default constructor for: TextBox
in default constructor for: Rect        <-- for tbox[1]
in default constructor for: Color
in default constructor for: TextBox
-->main() complete<--
in destructor for: TextBox              <-- for tbox[1]
in destructor for: Color
in destructor for: Rect
in destructor for: TextBox              <-- for tbox[0]
in destructor for: Color
in destructor for: Rect
```

The first three lines show the messages printed by the construction of tbox[0]. The next three show these messages for tbox[1]. After main() is completed, we see the messages printed by the destruction of tbox[1] and then tbox[0]. Most code does not depend on the order of construction and destruction of array elements, but the language does guarantee this order.

Implicit Default Constructors and Destructors

If you do not supply a default constructor or destructor for a class, the class will contain *implicit* ones. The implicit default constructor and destructor are equivalent to a default constructor and destructor with an empty body. They do nothing but chain to the default constructors and destructors of the class members that are class instances. For many classes, the implicit versions are just fine.

If you do declare a default constructor or destructor in the class body, you must define that member function as well. The compiler views a declaration as a promise that a definition exists. A declaration without a definition will result in a linker error if you try to instantiate the class. This error prevents surprises if you forget to link in the file with the default constructor or destructor's definition.

Private Constructors and Destructors

Like other member functions, constructors and destructors can be declared to be private. This limits how the class can be instantiated. It is useful for special classes that shouldn't be created or destroyed by just anyone. Note that implicit constructors and destructors are public.

Beyond Chaining

We've spent a lot of time talking about how default constructors automatically chain. Let's not lose sight of the big picture. The job of a default constructor is to put a class instance into a known default state. Part of this job is achieved by automatic chaining, that is, putting the class members into a known default state. But an object is more than the sum of its parts. The default constructor can perform tasks not handled by the construction of individual members.

The simplest example of what a constructor may need to handle is the print statement we've added to some default constructors announcing that a new object is
being constructed. More realistic examples include an object changing the default
value of one of its members, adding itself to some list, or drawing itself on the
screen. This other work is done in the constructor's body.

Similarly for the destructor, destroying individual class members might not be
enough. The destructor body should do what it takes to clean up after the object
as a whole. Chaining then ensures that individual class members clean up after
themselves. Only pointers are not able to handle their own cleanup.

So a simple declaration like:

```
main() {
    TextBox tbox;
    // ...
}
```

causes a lot of things to happen. First, the compiler ensures that memory for the
`TextBox` instance has been allocated, information needed by the run-time system
has been set up,* and all class members that are class instances have been default
constructed. Your default constructor body is then executed.

Between the time the constructor is exited and the destructor is entered, the object
exists as a whole. Remember that any function called from a constructor or
destructor is part of the construction or destruction process. Such a function
should not make assumptions about the state of the object that are not valid when
the object is not complete. It may assume that the class members that were
chained to are constructed. But it may not assume that the class as a whole is. See
Figure 6-2, which summarizes the lifetime of an object.

Explicit Invocation

Explicit invocation of a constructor is illegal and explicit invocation of a destructor
is an advanced topic:

```
main() {
    TextBox tbox;
    // ...
    tbox.TextBox();  // error: cannot explicitly invoke constructor
    // ...
    tbox.~TextBox(); // advanced topic: do not explicitly invoke destructor
    // ...
}
```

---

* We tell more about this in Chapter 12, *Polymorphism with Virtual Functions.*

> **❶ Before constructor body is entered, the compiler...**
> - Allocates object memory
> - Sets up run-time info
> - Chains, that is, invokes constructors for members that are class instances
>
> **❷ Inside constructor body, you should...**
> - Put class members that are instances of built-in types into a known state
> - Do any other tasks required by the object as a whole
>
> **❸ After constructor exits and before destructor is entered you...**
> - Use the object
>
> **❹ Inside destructor body you should...**
> - Complete any tasks required by the object as a whole
> - Free memory pointed to by pointer members
>
> **❺ After the destructor body is exited the compiler...**
> - Chains, that is, invokes destructors for members that are class instances
> - Frees object memory

Figure 6–2: Stages of an object's lifetime

We would not even bring this up, except there is one subtlety that can get you in trouble. You can use the syntax of an explicit constructor invocation, but it might not do what you expect. Say you want a `Point` class that has a `reset()` function to set it back to (0, 0). You might try to make `reset()` call the default constructor like this:

```
class Point {/*...*/ int x, y;}; // Point class with data members x and y
Point::Point() {x = y = 0;}      // default constructor sets Point to (0, 0)
Point::reset() {Point();}        // nice try, but does not reset Point
```

Instead of reinvoking the default constructor on an existing `Point`, this definition of `reset()` creates an entirely new, unnamed `Point` object, as if you had written:

```
Point::reset() {Point p1;}       // equivalent to reset() above
```

If you want to simulate the ability to invoke the constructor, simply put the code into another member function. You can call this from the constructor and from other code. Here, both the default constructor and `reset()` call the `init()` function:

```
Point::init()  {x = y = 0;}      // common construction code goes here
Point::Point() {init();}         // default constructor calls init()
Point::reset() {init();}         // reset() calls init()
```

Flow of Control

To ensure that objects are constructed correctly, C++ forbids jumping past an object's declaration to a point where the object is still in scope. In other words, if you jump past an object's declaration, you must jump past the end of the block containing that declaration.

Declarations Mixed with Statements

 These rules restricting the jumping of declarations become more important when you learn that, in C++, declarations don't have to come at the beginning of a block. You can write something like this:

```
main() {
    cout << "test: ";
    int i = 0;
    cout << i++ << '\n';
}
```

Here we declare i in the middle of a block, after we have already executed a statement. We can even declare variables in more unusual places, such as in a for loop like this:

```
main() {
    for (int i = 0; i < 3; i++)
        cout << i << '\n';
}
```

Putting declarations between statements allows you to declare a variable right before you use it.

This requirement doesn't affect most structured flow-of-control constructs like if and while or even break and continue. But it does restrict the goto and the switch. Here are uses of goto that are and are not allowed:

```
main() {
    if (test1) goto label1; // error: this goto skips over declaration of a1
    if (test2) goto label2; // ok: this goto skips entire block enclosing a1
    for(;;) {
        IntArray a1;
    label1:
        // ...
    }
label2:
    // ...
}
```

Jumping to label1 skips the declaration of a1 but not its enclosing block. This is illegal and the compiler will complain. Without the declaration of a1, this code would be strange, but legal. Jumping to label2 skips a1's entire enclosing block, so it is legal.

Here are uses of switch that are and are not allowed:

```
switch (value) {
    IntArray a1;      // error: declaration jumped, but not entire block
case value1:
    {
        IntArray a2; // ok: when declaration jumped, entire block jumped
        // ...         //      because of braces
        break;
    }
    // ...
}
```

No matter what case is chosen, the declaration of a1 is skipped, but its enclosing block is not. This is illegal. The declaration of a2 does not cause such problems. If some case other than the one shown is chosen, a2's entire enclosing block is skipped; this is allowed.

Time of Invocation

Occasionally, it is not so obvious when an object is constructed and destroyed, so we'll spend some time on this issue. An object can be:

- Automatic local

- Static local

- Global

- Dynamic

The next four sections describe construction and destruction for objects in each of these categories.[*]

Before we proceed, note that C++ forbids the compiler to optimize out an unused object whose constructor or destructor has a side effect. So even if an object is not used, its constructor and destructor will be called when you expect it to be.

---

[*] An object can also be a compiler-generated temporary. We discuss this further in Chapter 8, *References*.

Automatic Local Objects

An automatic local object is constructed each time control passes through its declaration. It is destroyed each time control passes back above its declaration or out of its enclosing block. Consider objects a1, a2, and a3 in this example:

```
void func() {              // each time function called:
    IntArray a1;               // a1 constructed here 1 time
    int i;
    for (i = 0; i < 3; i++) {
        IntArray a2;           // a2 constructed here 3 times
        if (i == 1) {
            IntArray a3;       // a3 constructed here 1 time
            // ...
        }                      // a3 destroyed here when "if" taken
    }                          // a2 destroyed here after each iteration
}                              // a1 destroyed here
```

Here a1 is constructed at the beginning of func() and destroyed when func() returns. In between, a2 is constructed and destroyed once for each of the three iterations of the for loop. During the second iteration, the if is taken and a3's constructor and destructor are invoked. Automatic locals are destroyed after a return statement, but not if exit() is called.

Static Local Objects

Like an automatic local, a static local is constructed when control passes through its declaration, but only the first time. It won't be constructed if control never passes through its declaration. If constructed, a static local is destroyed when the program exits normally, that is, when main() returns or exit() is called. For example in this code:

```
void func() {
    static IntArray a1;     // a1 constructed here first time through
    if (test) {
        static IntArray a2; // a2 constructed here first time "if" taken
        // ...
    }
}                           // if constructed, destroyed on normal program exit
```

a1 is constructed the first time func() is called, while a2 is constructed the first time the if test succeeds. If the program exits normally, a1 is destroyed if func() was ever called, and a2 is destroyed if the if ever succeeded.

Global Objects

Because constructors aren't invoked until run-time, construction of globals is an example of dynamic initialization as discussed in Chapter 2, *C++ Without Classes*. In that chapter you learned that globals are typically dynamically initialized before main() is entered. You also learned that, in a single translation unit, globals are initialized in the order they are defined; between translation units, however, you cannot depend on the order of global initialization.

This ordering is only important if the constructor of one global refers to another global that might not have already been constructed. For instance, here the constructor for MyClass writes to the global object myStdout:

```
// in my_stdio.h
class MyFile {/*...*/};
extern MyFile myStdout; // defined in my_stdio.cc

// in my_prog.cc
#include "my_stdio.h"
class MyClass {/*...*/};
MyClass::MyClass() {myStdout.write("in MyClass default constructor\n");}
MyClass myObject; // dangerous: will myStdout be constructed before myObject?
```

This code will fail if myObject is constructed before myStdout, because myObject's constructor uses myStdout. The user of myObject might not even be aware that its constructor accesses a global defined in another translation unit. A similar problem can occur if the MyClass destructor refers to myStdout.

You can avoid this ordering problem in your code by not referring, in your constructors and destructors, to globals defined in other translation units. It's usually safe to use globals defined in libraries like *iostream*, however, because library writers can use advanced techniques to prevent order dependencies from being a problem.

Globals that were constructed are destroyed when the program exits normally. They are destroyed in the reverse order of construction.

Dynamic Objects

The final type of object is a dynamic object. In C you create and destroy dynamic objects with malloc() and free(), respectively. But calls to malloc() and free() are not sufficient to create dynamic class instances in C++. Those functions handle raw memory. We need to ensure that an object is constructed and destroyed correctly. How to create and destroy dynamic objects is covered in the next chapter.

7

Better Abstraction with new and delete

Containers—such as arrays, linked lists, and trees—require dynamic memory. In C, you typically use the functions `malloc()` and `free()` for dynamic memory. C++ uses two new keywords: `new` and `delete`.

Why didn't C++ stick with `malloc()` and `free()`? Because they only allocate and deallocate memory. C++ needs to create and destroy objects, which are much more than just memory. C++ must ensure, for example, that an object's constructor and destructor are called.

C++ distinguishes between dynamic objects and dynamic arrays of objects. The operators `new` and `delete` create and destroy dynamic objects. The operators `new[]` and `delete[]` create and destroy dynamic arrays of objects.[*] Both pairs of operators are covered in this chapter.

Dynamic Objects

Allocation and deallocation of memory for an object in C looks like this:

```
Mytype *ptr = malloc(sizeof(Mytype));
/* use ptr... */
free(ptr);
```

Creation and destruction of a dynamic object in C++ looks like this:

```
Mytype *ptr = new Mytype;
// use ptr...
delete ptr;
```

---

[*] These can be called the *new/delete-object* and the *new/delete-array* operators.

The new operator is followed by the type of object to create. new allocates memory for the object and invokes the object's default constructor. The result is a pointer to the object created. The delete operator takes a pointer to the object to be destroyed. delete invokes the object's destructor and frees its memory. You can safely delete the null pointer. Note that the new operator doesn't need parentheses around the type, and the delete operator doesn't need them around the pointer.

You can use the new and delete operators to create dynamic instances of both classes and built-in types. For classes, you must always use the new and delete operators, rather than malloc() and free(), to ensure that dynamic class instances are created and destroyed correctly. No constructors or destructors are called when you use new and delete on built-in types, however. So it doesn't matter whether you use them or stick with malloc() and free().

The new operator can take any type, even complicated ones:

```
// allocate a pointer to character
char **ptr = new char*;

// allocate a pointer to a function which takes an int and returns a double
double (**f)(int) = new (double (*)(int));
```

When the type has parentheses in it, as in the last example above, you need parentheses around the whole type or it will parse incorrectly:

```
f = new double (*)(int);      // error: type needs parentheses to parse correctly
f = new (double (*)(int));    // correct
```

Dynamic Arrays

Allocation and deallocation of memory for an array in C looks like this:

```
int howmany;
Mytype *array;
/* ... */
array = malloc(sizeof(Mytype) * howmany);
/* ... */
free(array);
```

Creation and destruction of a dynamic array of objects in C++ looks like this:

```
int howmany;
Mytype *array;
// ...
array = new Mytype[howmany];
// ...
delete[] array;
```

The new[] operator takes the type of the array's elements and the number of elements. It allocates space for the entire array, then calls the default constructor for each of the array elements in order of increasing index. It results in a pointer to the first element of the array. You can allocate an array with zero elements and you'll get back a non-null pointer.

The `delete[]` operator calls the destructor for each of the array elements in the opposite order they were constructed, and then deallocates the memory. You can safely `delete[]` the null pointer.

We call it the `new[]` operator even though the brackets are not next to the keyword `new`. This syntax is easy to understand with simple examples like the one above. It can be more challenging with complicated types, where the brackets of `new[]` are buried in the middle of the type:

```
// allocate an array of pointers to functions
double (**f)(int) = new (double (*[10])(int));
```

You might think that you can generalize the syntax to allocate a dynamic, multidimensional array. You can't with `new[]`. Here are some examples of what you can and can't do:

```
int i, j, k;
Mytype *a0 = new Mytype;           // ok: dynamic object created with new
Mytype *a1 = new Mytype[i];        // ok: dynamic 1d array created with new[]
Mytype **a2 = new Mytype[i][j];    // error: dynamic 2d array not allowed
Mytype ***a3 = new Mytype[i][j][k]; // error: dynamic 3d array not allowed
```

In this example, the first `new` creates a dynamic `Mytype` object and the second creates a dynamic one-dimensional array of such objects. The last two try to create dynamic multidimensional arrays and will fail with compilation errors.

You *can* create a dynamic array of pointers that can then point to other dynamic arrays:

```
Mytype **a2 = new Mytype*[i];    // ok: dynamic array of pointers
Mytype ***a3 = new Mytype**[i]; // ok: dynamic array of pointers to pointers
```

Here a2 points to an array of pointers to `Mytype`. Using a loop, you can make each pointer element point to its own array, creating a dynamic two-dimensional array. Using two nested loops, you can make a3 point to a dynamic three-dimensional array.

Alternatively, you can create a dynamic array of static arrays:

```
Mytype (*a2)[6] = new Mytype[i][6];       // ok: dyn array of static 1d array
Mytype (*a3)[7][8] = new Mytype[i][7][8]; // ok: dyn array of static 2d array
```

In this example a2 points to a two-dimensional array whose number of rows is dynamic, but whose number of columns is always six. Similarly, a3 points to a three-dimensional array with one dynamic and two static dimensions.

The moral is that new[], like new, takes a type. This means that all dimensions except the first must be compile-time constants. Notice that the types of a2 and a3 in the last example above include the sizes of these static dimensions. A typedef clarifies the syntax:

```
typedef Mytype Mytype78[7][8];  // typedef to make code clearer
Mytype78 *a3 = new Mytype78[i]; // identical to last line of previous example
```

Now that we've hidden the extra brackets with a typedef, we see that the last line of the previous example reduces to a simple new[].

Mixing Allocators

A common mistake is to forget the brackets when you mean to delete[] a dynamic array:

```
Mytype *array = new Mytype[10];
// ...
delete array;    // wrong: this delete needs brackets because we used new[]
```

The compiler cannot catch this mistake because C++, like C, does not distinguish between a pointer to an object and a pointer to an array of objects. The result of this mistake is undefined, but could be a crash or heap corruption.

The result of delete[]ing a pointer to a non-array is also undefined. For example,

```
int *single = new int;
// ...
delete[] single;   // wrong: brackets shouldn't be there because we used new
```

These easy-to-make mistakes are among the reasons why we recommend you use an array class instead of built-in arrays when possible.

You can use both new/delete[*] and malloc()/free() in the same program, but you must not free() a pointer returned by new, and you must not delete a pointer returned by malloc(). The compiler doesn't catch these errors, so you can end up with difficult bugs to track down. Watch out.

realloc()

If new replaces malloc(), it's reasonable to wonder what replaces realloc(). Unfortunately, C++ does not provide a replacement for realloc(). Remember, you can still use malloc() for built-in types. When you use malloc(), you can still use realloc().

---

* From now on, you can assume what we say about new and delete holds for new[] and delete[] as well.

Memory Management
with new and delete

To allocate the needed memory, the new operator actually invokes a function called operator new(). You can override this function to handle memory allocation yourself. You could, for example, allocate memory for certain objects in a very fast way. You can also overload this function and pass special parameters through the new operator. For instance, you might have a number of heaps and want to specify which one to use:

```
Foo *f = new(my_heap) Foo;
```

Here we see new followed by the heap to place the object in.

The delete operator similarly invokes operator delete() to free the memory. This function can be overridden but not overloaded like operator new().

You cannot realloc() an object created with new or an array created with new[]. To increase the size of a C++ array allocated with new[], you must do the realloc() yourself. That is, you must create a new array, copy the old values to the new array, then destroy the old array. Array classes often can do this for you.

You can continue to use other memory functions—calloc(), alloca(), etc.—on built-in types allocated with malloc(). You must not, however, use them with classes.

Out of Memory

If the new operator cannot allocate the needed memory, it invokes the function indicated by a pointer called the *new-handler*. This function could simply print an error message and exit, or free some memory and return. If this function returns, new again tries to allocate the requested memory. This continues until the memory is available or the new-handler exits.

If the new-handler is null (its default value), new does one of two things, depending on how up-to-date your compiler is. Traditionally, a null new-handler means that new returns the null pointer when memory is exhausted, just as malloc() does. More recently, if the new-handler is null, new terminates the program.[*]

---

[*] This may seem like a step backwards from the original behavior of new. In truth, when the new-handler is null, new does something more sophisticated than terminating the program. What it does exactly is covered in the "Exceptions" box below.

Exceptions

The actual default behavior of new when it cannot allocate memory involves *exceptions*. Exceptions are a sophisticated error-handling technique new to C++. They address this problem: code that encounters an error usually does not know how to handle it. Exceptions allow an error to propagate up to code that does know how to handle it. Intermediate levels, between where the error is found and where it is handled, don't need to worry about checking for the error.

When a routine finds a serious problem, the routine can *throw* an object representing the exception. Execution resumes at the first level up the function-call chain that is prepared to *catch* the exception object. On the way up the call chain, destructors are invoked when necessary. Code tells what exception objects it is prepared to handle with a *try-block*. Here is a simple example:

```
void thrower() {
    // ...
    if (error_found)
        throw "major bummer"; // throw an exception
    // ...
}

void catcher() {
    // ...
    try {                      // prepare for exceptions in following code
        // ...
        thrower();
        // ...
    }
    catch (char *str) {        // catch an exception from previous code
        // handle exception
    }
    // ...
}
```

If thrower() finds an error, it throws the string "major bummer". This will be caught and handled by thrower()'s caller catcher(). Uncaught exceptions cause program termination. So, because a null new-handler causes new to throw an exception that beginner's code does not catch, memory exhaustion seems to the beginner to simply terminate the program.

To change the value of the new-handler, you invoke a function called
set_new_handler().* It is declared in the header *new.h* and looks something like
this:

```
typedef void (*PFV)();              // useful typedef
extern PFV set_new_handler(PFV);    // declaration of set_new_handler()
```

You pass it a pointer to the function to call when memory is exhausted, or the null
pointer. It returns the previous value of the new-handler. Any function assigned to
the new-handler must take no parameters and return no value. Here we set the
new-handler three times:

```
#include <new.h>              // declares set_new_handler()
void my_handler() {/*...*/}   // our own special handler

main() {
    void (*old_handler)();    // holds old setting of new-handler
                              // if memory cannot be allocated, new will...
    // ...                                     // default: terminate program
    old_handler = set_new_handler(my_handler);  // now: call my_handler()
    old_handler = set_new_handler(old_handler); // now: terminate program again
    old_handler = set_new_handler(old_handler); // now: call my_handler() again
}
```

When the program begins, the new-handler is null. We first set the new-handler to
our own function, my_handler(); then we set the new-handler back to its default
value which we stored in old_handler; finally we again set it to call my_handler().

Remember that dynamic initialization of globals occurs before main() runs. So setting the value of the new-handler as the first line of main() may not be soon
enough to catch memory exhaustion. For example, this code uses the default
value of the new-handler if memory is not available for piggy_array:

```
void my_handler() {/*...*/}          // our own special handler
int *piggy_array = new int[1000000]; // executed before main() runs

main() {
    void (*old_handler)()
        = set_new_handler(my_handler); // executed after piggy_array is init
    // ...
}
```

Here we set the new-handler to my_handler() in the first line of main(). Before this
runs, however, the global piggy_array is initialized by requesting lots of dynamic
memory. If this allocation fails, my_handler() will not be called because we have
not yet assigned it to the new-handler.

---

* At least one compiler we've seen calls this function _set_new_handler() with an underscore at the beginning. This is not standard, but you may run into it.

To catch memory exhaustion sooner, you must call set_new_handler() as part of the initialization of some global:

```
void my_handler() {/*...*/}        // our own special handler
void (*old_handler)()
    = set_new_handler(my_handler); // executed before piggy_array init
int *piggy_array = new int[10000]; // executed after set_new_handler() called

main() {
    // ...
}
```

Here old_handler is global, so this code calls set_new_handler() before initializing piggy_array. You don't need to worry about invoking set_new_handler() this soon if you don't allocate lots of memory while initializing globals.

8

References

As we saw in Chapter 6, *Better Abstraction with Constructors and Destructors*, the default constructor and the destructor take no parameters and return no values. Other special member functions, which we introduce in the next chapter, do require parameters and return values. They, however, pass this information in a new way, using references, which we introduce in this chapter. We'll first review passing by value, as you've done in C; then we'll explain the new way of passing information using references; finally we'll talk about some limits and problems with this new way of passing information. Along the way we'll try to distinguish between references and their cousins, pointers.

Parameter Versus Argument

Before we proceed, we need to briefly discuss terminology. Typically, the word *parameter* refers to both a value passed to a function and to the variable inside the function that receives that value. Some people use the adjectives *actual* and *formal*, respectively, to distinguish the two kinds of parameters. We find this cumbersome and choose to use a more informal distinction. We call the value passed an *argument* and the variable inside the function that receives it a *parameter*, as this example illustrates:

```
main() {
    print_it(5);        // we call 5 an "argument"
}
```

```
void print_it(int i) { // we call i a "parameter"
    printf("%d", i);    // here parameter i is an argument to another function
}
```

Passing by Value in C and C++

In C, all arguments are passed by *value.*[*] This means that, when the function is called, the value of the argument is copied into the parameter. After that, the argument and the parameter have no relationship. In particular, changing the parameter does not change the argument:

```
void func1(int i) {    // func1() takes an int by value
    // ...
    i = 5;             // i is now 5
    // ...
}

main() {
    int n = 3;         // n is 3 before call to func1()
    func1(n);          // n passed by value to func1()
    // ...             // n is still 3 after func1() returns
}
```

Here n is passed by value to the function func1(). Changing the parameter i does not affect the argument n. If we want a function to alter an argument, we must pass a pointer to it:

```
void func2(int *pi) { // func2() takes an int by pointer
    // ...
    *pi = 5;          // what pi points to is now 5
    // ...
}
main() {
    int n = 3;        // n is 3 before call to func2()
    func2(&n);        // n passed by pointer to func2()
    // ...            // n is 5 after func2() returns
}
```

Here n is passed by pointer to function func2(). We change n through the pointer pi. Passing by pointer is also used to avoid copying a large object when passing it to a function:

```
void func3(BigClass *b) { // func3() takes a BigClass by pointer
    // ...
}

main() {
    BigClass bb;
```

---

* Note that parameter passing using a pointer is really still passing by value. We are simply passing the pointer by value.

```
        func3 (&bb);              // bb passed by pointer to func3()
        // ...
    }
```

Here bb is passed by pointer to function func3(). Though we may have no intention of altering bb in func3(), passing it by pointer saves us execution time by avoiding a copy of all of bb's data.

Passing by Reference in C++

You will usually pass parameters by value in C++, but at times you need to pass them by *reference*. This is a form of parameter passing that is new to C++. When passing by reference, the argument is not copied. Instead, the parameter becomes an *alias* for the argument. That is, the argument and parameter refer to the same area of storage. If you alter the parameter, you are altering the argument. This may sound a lot like passing by pointer. Passing by reference is very similar to passing by pointer, but look at this example:

```
    void func4(int &ri) { // func4() takes an int by reference (note the ampersand)
        // ...
        ri = 5;           // assign 5 to ri
        // ...
    }

    main() {
        int n = 3;        // n is 3 before call to func4()
        func4(n);         // n passed by reference to func4()
        // ...            // n is 5 after func4() returns
    }
```

The ampersand (&) in the declaration of ri turns it into a reference parameter rather than a value parameter. When the function func4() is called, ri is said to be *bound* to n. Once ri is bound, it cannot be distinguished from a normal int. For the duration of the function, ri and n are two names for the same object. (Of course, inside func4(), only the name ri is in scope.) So setting ri to five inside func4() actually sets n to five. In addition, if you take the address of the parameter ri, you get the address of the argument n. Consider this program:

```
    int n;

    void func5(int &ri) {
        if (&ri == &n) cout << "you passed n\n";
    }

    main() {
        func5(n);
    }
```

Here func5() takes an int by reference. It compares the address of the parameter ri to the address of the global n and prints a message if they are the same. When main() calls func5() with n, the function will print the message. Once ri is bound to n, they refer to the same object.

You can pass any type by reference. Here we pass a class:

```
void inc_each(IntArray &array) {
    size_t i;
    for (i = 0; i < array.getNumElems(); i++)
        array.setElem(i, array.getElem(i)+1);
}

main() {
    IntArray grades;
    // ...
    inc_each(grades);
}
```

The function inc_each() takes an IntArray by reference. It increments each element of the array by one. Note that inside inc_each(), the parameter array is treated like a regular class. Only by looking at array's declaration can we see that it is a reference parameter and not a value parameter. When main() calls inc_each(), the argument grades and the parameter array are two names for the same IntArray object.(Only the name array is valid, though, within inc_each().)

Reference Versus Pointer

As we said, references are closely related to pointers.[*] In fact, you can think of references as special kinds of pointers: pointers that don't need explicit pointer syntax. Compare these function definitions and invocations:

```
void func_ptr(int *pi) {*pi = 5;} // must dereference pi to alter i
void func_ref(int &ri) {ri = 5;}  // can alter i without dereference
main() {
    int i;
    func_ptr(&i); // explicitly pass address of i
    func_ref(i);  // just pass i
}
```

Here func_ptr() takes a pointer to an int and func_ref() takes a reference to an int. We pass i to each of them. When we call func_ptr(), we need to explicitly take the address of i. When we call func_ref(), we can just pass i itself. Both functions alter i: func_ptr() needs to dereference parameter pi; func_ref() simply needs to assign to parameter ri. Note how a few more ampersands and

---

[*] It's actually quite likely that the compiler translates passing by reference into passing by pointer behind the scenes.

asterisks are required to handle the pointer, while a reference can generally be treated as a normal object except for its declaration.

References were not introduced into the language to save a few keystrokes, however. They were introduced because sometimes abstraction requires C++ to invoke functions without the user explicitly knowing that a function is being called. We saw this with the default constructor: a simple declaration can actually invoke a slew of function calls. C++ needs a way to pass large objects as arguments to these "secret" function calls without requiring the user to explicitly pass the address. We'll see examples of this in the next chapter.

The ampersand declaring a reference has the same syntax and precedence as the asterisk does when used to declare a pointer. Here are a few sample declarations:

```
void func(SomeType &s);        // s is a reference to a SomeType
void func(SomeType *&s);        // s is a reference to a pointer to a SomeType
void func(SomeType (*&s)());    // s is a reference to a ptr to a function taking
                                //      no parameters and returning a SomeType
```

At first the ampersand may seem to be an odd way to represent references. It takes a bit of mental juggling, but eventually it makes sense. We think of it as saying that the parameter takes the address of objects for you.

Another important similarity between pointers and references involves casting to base classes. Recall from Chapter 5, *Hierarchy with Composition and Derivation*, that the compiler lets you access the base-class part of a derived-class object by converting a derived-class pointer to a base-class pointer. So if you have a hierarchy like this:

```
class Base {/*...*/};
class Derived : public Base {/*...*/};
```

you can do something like this:

```
void func(Base *pbase);
main() {
    Derived deriv;
    // ...
    func(&deriv); // during this function invocation pbase points to the
}                 // base-class part of deriv
```

Here we pass a pointer to `deriv`, a `Derived` instance, to `func()`, which takes a `Base` pointer. The compiler automatically points the parameter `pbase` to the `Base` part of `deriv`.

Similarly, a reference can bind to the base-class part of a derived-class object:

```
void func(Base &rbase);
main() {
    Derived deriv;
```

```
// ...
func(deriv);    // during this function invocation rbase refers to the
                // base-class part of deriv
}
```

We can pass `deriv` to `func()` even though the function takes a `Base` reference. The compiler automatically binds the parameter `rbase` to the `Base` part of argument `deriv`.

Arguably, there is one more similarity between pointers and references. Recall the trouble you had first understanding pointers or, on a more positive note, the thrill of comprehension you received when you finally understood how to use them. Well, references allow you to relive that moment of insight all over again. Don't be discouraged if they confuse you at first.

Returning by Reference in C++

Passing by reference can also be used in the other direction to create a return by reference. Here's a function, `getTbox()`, that returns a reference to a global, `globalTbox`:

```
TextBox globalTbox;
TextBox &getTbox() {return globalTbox;}      // return by reference
```

The ampersand says that the result of `getTbox()` is a reference to a `TextBox` instance. This means if you write:

```
getTbox().setColor(BLUE);
```

the color of the global `globalTbox` is set to BLUE. If we had written the return value of `getTbox()` without the ampersand—creating the typical return by value—the color of a *copy* of `globalTbox` would be changed by the above expression.

We purposely showed `getTbox()` returning a global by reference. You cannot return an automatic local by reference because it ceases to exist when the function returns:

```
int &func() {
    int loc = 5;    // automatic local
    return loc;     // error: returning automatic local by reference
}

main() {
    cout << func() << '\n';    // what number prints is undefined
}
```

The function `func()` returns a reference to `loc`, an automatic local. But `loc` no longer exists when `func()` exits. We thus have a reference to garbage. If you run this program, you cannot be sure what value will print.

We can make this code work by dropping the ampersand to make func() return by value:

```
int func() {
    int loc = 5;       // automatic local
    return loc;        // ok: returning automatic local by value
}
```

In this case, the compiler copies the value of loc into a temporary location so the function caller can access it. If we really want func() to return by reference, however, we can change loc to static:

```
int &func() {
    static int loc = 5; // static local
    return loc;         // ok: returning static local by reference
}
```

In this case, loc exists after the function exits, so we have no problem returning a reference to it.

In this final example, func() can be used anywhere an int is allowed. For example, we can assign to it like this:

```
main() {
    func() = 1066;     // assigns to local static loc
}
```

This assignment changes loc to 1066 because func() returns loc by reference. If func() returned loc by value, this assignment would be illegal. In that case, we would be trying to change the value of a temporary generated by the compiler to hold the return value.

Overloading: Reference Versus Value

Because passing by value and by reference look identical to the caller, you cannot overload a function based only on whether a parameter is a value or reference. Here we have created two versions of func(): one taking a value parameter, the other taking a reference parameter:

```
void func(Foo f);  // can't have both of these functions
void func(Foo &f); // their signatures do not differ enough

main() {
    Foo ff;
    func(ff);      // which should be invoked?
}
```

If both versions of func() were allowed, the compiler would not know which to invoke inside main(). So the compiler doesn't allow it.

References in Other Contexts

References need not only be parameters or return values. They can be regular variables:

```
main() {
    int i;
    int &ri = i; // ri is an alias for i
    ri = 5;      // assigns 5 to i
    // ...
}
```

References can even be class members or the target of a cast. Because references were added to the language to aid passing information between functions, using references in places other than function parameters and returns doesn't add much that you can't do with pointers.

Binding Problems

We often take for granted that the compiler generates intermediate temporaries for us. For instance, when you cast a `long` to an `int`, the compiler usually creates an invisible `int` variable to hold the result. These temporaries can be a problem with references because the compiler does not bind references to the temporaries it generates. It assumes that, if the reference is altered, you want to see the alteration, not have it go away with the temporary.

In practice this limitation means the compiler complains if you try to pass the wrong type, an expression result, or a literal. Here are some examples showing what is not allowed:

```
void func(int &ri);  // function takes a reference to an int
main() {
    int int_var;
    long long_var;

    func(int_var);    // ok: passing an int variable
    func(long_var);   // error: passing a long variable
    func(int_var*2);  // error: passing an expression result
    func(5);          // error: passing a literal
}
```

In this example, `func()` takes a reference to an `int`. The first invocation of `func()` passes the `int` variable `int_var`, which is fine. The next three invocations should not be allowed by the compiler. They all would require `ri` to bind to a compiler-generated temporary.

The compiler also generates a temporary when a function returns by value, like val_func() does here:

```
int val_func() { // function returns by value (temporary generated)
    int i = 5; return i; }

int &ref_func() {      // function returns by reference (no temp generated)
    static int i = 5;
    return i;
}

void func(int &ri);    // function takes a reference to an int
main() {
    func(val_func());  // error: passing return by value
    func(ref_func());  // ok: passing return by reference
}
```

Here the compiler needs to generate a temporary to hold the value returned by val_func(). You cannot pass this result by reference. Because ref_func() returns a reference, no temporary is generated and you may pass this result by reference.

To fix the errors shown above, simply assign the value to an object of the correct type and then pass that object:

```
main() {
    int n;
    // ...
    n = 5;          // assign literal to variable
    func(n);        // ok: passing a variable by reference

    n = val_func(); // assign return by value to variable
    func(n);        // ok: passing a variable by reference
}
```

These invocations of func() are legal because we have assigned the literal 5 and the value returned by val_func() to the variable n. We then pass n by reference. You could also assign a long or an expression to n, to solve the other errors shown two examples above.

9

Better Abstraction with Other Special Member Functions

In Chapter 6, *Better Abstraction with Constructors and Destructors*, we saw member functions that help with:

* Initialization of the object from scratch (default constructor)

* Clean up of the object (destructor)

This chapter describes three more member functions that help you create better abstractions. These member functions help with:

* Assignment to the object (assignment operator)

* Initialization of the object based on another object (copy constructor)

* Printing the object (printing member function)

Each of these member functions is covered in its own section below. While covering assignment and printing, we'll also see the two most common uses of operator overloading in C++.

As with the default constructor and destructor, you must understand how the member functions we discuss here interact with class hierarchy. We will use the class hierarchy introduced in Chapter 6. A `TextBox` is derived from a `Rect` and has three data members. One data member is of class `Color`; another is an `int`; and the last is a `char*`.

```
// recall this hierarchy from a previous chapter
class Rect {
    // ...
private:
    int top, left;
    int width, height;
};
```

```
class Color {
    // ...
private:
    int data;
};

class TextBox : public Rect {
    // ...
private:
    Color textColor;
    int frameThickness;
    char *text;
};
```

Assignment Operator

The first member function we cover, the assignment operator, allows you to assign instances of a class to each other using a standard assignment statement:

```
main() {
    TextBox source, destination;
    // ...
    destination = source;    // assigning one TextBox instance to another
}
```

For C structs, assignment is defined as copying the bits making up source into destination. This is often not adequate for objects in C++. Consider the example shown in Figure 9-1, which shows the assignment of one TextBox instance to another as if they were C structs. Given the data shown under "Before Assignment," assignment of source to destination results in the data shown under "After Assignment."

After the assignment shown in this figure, source and destination both point to the same string "hi". This causes a problem if one of them changes this string. One object might even free the string in its destructor before the other object is done with it. In addition, the string "lo" that destination pointed to has been lost without being freed—a memory leak.

C programmers accept that the assignment operator cannot be used with most structs. They usually create a function called something like copy() to handle assignment in these cases. But in C++, you can use the syntax of assignment and get the flexibility of a copy() function call. To do this, you add a member function like the one shown in this class declaration:

```
class TextBox {
public:
    void operator=(TextBox &source); // invoked by assignment
    //...                            // note reference parameter
};
```

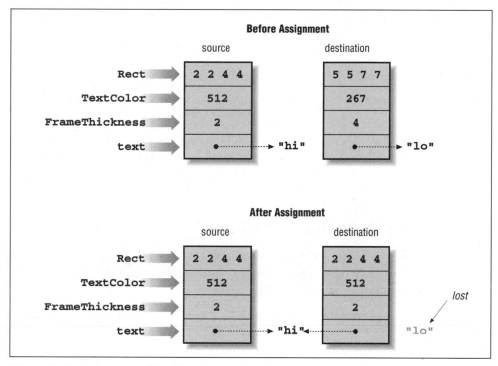

Figure 9-1: Assignment of TextBox instances in C

The name of this new member function is operator=, that is, the keyword operator followed by the assignment operator. It is called the *assignment operator member function* or, more simply, the *assignment operator*. This function takes a single parameter: a reference to an object of the class to which the function is a member. This function is invoked when you assign one TextBox to another:

```
main() {
    TextBox source, destination;
    // ...
    destination = source;    // invokes TextBox::operator=()
}
```

The final line of main() invokes TextBox::operator=() on the object destination with source as the argument. This assignment statement is actually a function call. Note that this function TextBox::operator=(TextBox &) takes a reference parameter. We don't want the user to have to explicitly take the address of source, nor do we want to pass it by value. Using a reference parameter allows us to assign classes using the same syntax as built-in types without the overhead of copying them as value parameters.

Do not be confused by the strange name and unusual way of invoking the assignment operator member function; it is a function like any other. If you like, you can invoke it like an ordinary member function:

```
main() {
    TextBox source, destination;
    // ...
    destination.operator=(source);    // we can invoke assignment operator
}                                     // like this, but usually do not
```

Here we use standard member function syntax to invoke the assignment operator. This is equivalent to the previous example in all ways, except perhaps in ease of understanding. You will see below that sometimes you must use this explicit function syntax.

Definition of Assignment Operator

We're now ready to define our own assignment operator for TextBox. We need to assign all the members, remembering to give text its own memory. Here is a definition that does this:

```
void TextBox::operator=(TextBox &source) {    // definition of TextBox asgn op
    // 1: don't assign to self
    if (this == &source) return;

    // 2: chain to base class assignment operator
    Rect::operator=(source);

    // 3: chain to data members' assignment operator
    textColor = source.textColor;
    frameThickness = source.frameThickness

    // 4: manage memory and assign to pointer member
    delete[] text;
    if (source.text != 0) {
        text = new char[strlen(source.text)+1];
        strcpy(text, source.text);
    }
    else {
        text = 0;
    }
}
```

The code in this example breaks down into four groups, which we have labeled with comments. Group 1 aborts the assignment if the source and destination are the same. We check for self-assignment by comparing the address of source to this, the address of the destination. Not only is this a simple optimization, it avoids the catastrophe of freeing memory and then using it in group 4 below. Assignment to self is quite possible, even in good code; it's a good idea to check for it.

Group 2 assigns the base-class (Rect) part of the source to the destination. This is done by chaining to the Rect assignment operator, that is, letting the base-class part of the object assign itself. We need to qualify the function name with Rect:: because both the Rect base class and the TextBox-derived class have an operator=() function. (We first discussed name qualification in Chapter 5, *Hierarchy with Composition and Derivation*.) If we tried to write:

```
operator=(source);     // not equivalent to group 2 above
```

we would have invoked TextBox::operator=() recursively. We could have used a standard assignment statement if we used casts:

```
*(Rect*)this = *(Rect*)&source;   // equivalent to group 2, but ugly and unsafe
```

Here we assign the Rect part by casting the source and destination to their Rect parts. This works in this example, but it is ugly. More importantly, casting is unsafe and should be avoided if a better solution exists.

Note that Rect::operator=(Rect &) takes a reference to a Rect, but the invocation above, Rect::operator=(source), passes a TextBox. This is OK because, as we discussed in the automatic pointer conversion section of Chapter 8, *References*, a reference can bind to the base-class part of a derived-class object. So we can pass a TextBox instance where a Rect reference is expected, and the compiler will bind the reference correctly.

Group 3 assigns the corresponding textColor and frameThickness data members. For most data members this is all we need to do. Their own assignment operators take care of the details. Note that group 2 and group 3 are very similar in all but their syntax. Group 2 chains to the base-class assignment operator. Group 3 chains to the data members' assignment operator. For built-in types in group 3 (like frameThickness in our example), chaining to the data members' assignment operator simply means using the built-in assignment, which copies the bits.

Group 4 copies the string between the text data members (using new[] and delete[] now that you have learned them). We must first free the old string in the destination before allocating memory and copying the new string from the source. This is how pointer data members are usually handled during assignment. We typically must free the old memory and then allocate and assign new memory.

We can make the assignment operator do anything we want. We could define it as:

```
void TextBox::operator=(TextBox &source) {
    cout << "forget it, I'm not assigning anything\n";
}
```

This simply prints an irritating message every time we try to assign one TextBox to another. It does nothing even vaguely like assignment. Though this is not recommended, the compiler won't complain.

Fancy Assignment

The assignment operator is actually more flexible than we show here. It can take a parameter of any type, be overloaded, etc. Defining an assignment operator that can be used with expressions like a = b = c is also possible. This requires the assignment operator to return a value that can be passed to the next assignment operator.

Implicit Assignment Operator

If you do not declare an assignment operator for a class, the class contains an implicit one. The implicit assignment operator simply chains to the assignment operators of the class members. This is often called *member-wise* assignment. Instances of built-in types assign by copying the bits from the source to the destination—*bitwise* assignment. That means pointer members are copied as shown in Figure 9-1, which would be unacceptable for this class.

If you declare an assignment operator in the class, you must define it, or you will get a linker error if you try to invoke it. Classes without pointer members can often get away with the implicit assignment operator. The class Rect, for example, can use its implicit version:

```
class Rect {            // use implicit assignment operator
    // no need to define assignment operator
    // ...
private:
    int left, top;
    int width, height;
};
```

The implicit assignment operator for Rect copies the four data members, which is exactly what we want. If, however, we add a uniqueId field to identify each Rect, we might not be able to use the implicit assignment operator:

```
class Rect {            // cannot use implicit assignment operator
    void operator=(Rect &src);
    // ...
private
    int left, top;
    int width, height;
    int uniqueId;       // different for every Rect
};
```

When assigning `Rects`, we do not want this field copied; so we must override the implicit assignment operator to prevent this. No user's code would have to change to take advantage of this new assignment, however. That is the beauty of good abstraction.

Unfortunately, there is no way to redefine assignment for just the members that need it. The implicit assignment operator chains to the assignment operator of *every* class member. The overriding assignment operator chains to *no* class member's assignment operator automatically. If chaining to every class member is not what you want, you need to handle the entire assignment.

Operator Overloading and References

Overriding the assignment operator is an example of an entire branch of C++ called *operator overloading*. Like function overloading, operator overloading allows the same operator to work on many different types. It is no accident that we introduced two large C++ topics—references and operator overloading—in back-to-back chapters. References were added to the language mainly to support operator overloading.

Because C++ implements operator overloading with function calls, sometimes objects are passed as arguments implicitly. Requiring objects to be passed as pointers in these circumstances would be awkward and copying them would be slow. You cannot be expected to write `dest = src` when assignment is predefined and `dest = &src` when you override it. This would defeat the abstraction that operator overloading is designed to create.

More Operator Overloading

Only a few operators work on class instances by default—e.g., `=` (assignment) and unary `&` (address-of). Operator overloading allows you to redefine operators like `+` and `->` with class instances. In C++, you can, for example, create a `Time` class that has `+` defined without being limited to implementing `Time` as an `int`. You can even make an array class that uses brackets like a built-in array. In this chapter, we cover the two most common uses of operator overloading: the assignment operator, described above, and the printing operator, described below.

Copy Constructor

The *copy constructor* is the second member function we discuss in this chapter. In Chapter 6, we saw how a default constructor creates an object from scratch, putting it in some default state. Another possibility is to create an object based on another object, which is what a copy constructor does. For instance:

```
main() {
    TextBox t1;        // construct t1 from scratch
    TextBox t2 = t1; // construct t2 based on t1
    // ...
}
```

The second line of `main()` may look like an assignment, but this use of the assignment operator during a declaration is actually an *initialization*. There is little difference in C between assignment and initialization. They both just copy the bits in the source to the destination. In C++ the difference is important. Assignment changes the value of an object that has already been constructed. Initialization constructs a *new* object and gives it a value at the same time.

This kind of initialization could actually be implemented as a call to the default constructor followed by a call to the assignment operator.[*] This would truly make initialization indistinguishable from assignment. For a large object, however, it might be wasteful to put it into the default state only to immediately change that state. C++ optimizes this by adding a new constructor: the copy constructor. It looks like this:

```
class TextBox {
public:
    TextBox(TextBox &source);    // declaration of copy constructor
    //...                        // note reference parameter
};
```

The copy constructor is probably the subtlest member function in C++. It is a bit like the default constructor and a bit like the assignment operator. For example, it is named like the default constructor and takes a parameter like the assignment operator. The copy constructor is invoked when an object is constructed based on another object of the same class:

```
main() {
    TextBox t1;        // invokes default constructor
    TextBox t2 = t1; // invokes copy constructor
    t2 = t1;           // invokes assignment operator
}
```

---

[*] The direct predecessor to C++, C with Classes, actually implemented initialization this way.

Each line of this `main()` invokes a different member function of `TextBox`. The first invokes the default constructor; the third invokes the assignment operator. On the second line, `t2` is declared and assigned at the same time. This is handled by the copy constructor. We say that `t2` is *copy constructed*.

Constructors with Parameters

A class can actually have constructors that take any parameters you like. For instance, a string class might have these:

```
class String {
public:
    String();                            // default construct String
    String(String &src);                 // copy construct String
    String(char *src);                   // construct String
                                         // from built-in one
    String(char src[], size_t len); // construct String
                                         // from char array
    // ...
};
```

Each is useful in a different circumstance. Their invocation looks like this:

```
main() {
    String s1;              // invokes default constructor
    String s2 = s1;         // invokes copy constructor
    String s3("hello");     // invokes third constructor
    String s4("hello", 5); // invokes fourth constructor
    // ...
}
```

In this book, we show only the first two constructors: the default constructor and the copy constructor.

Defining the Copy Constructor

We now need to define the copy constructor. In this section, we're going to teach the easy way to define it, rather than the most efficient way. For now just worry about understanding what the copy constructor does and how it does it. The efficient way to implement the copy constructor in described in an advanced-topic box later in this chapter.

Like the default constructor defined in Chapter 6, the copy constructor automatically chains to the default constructors of the class members that are class instances. So when the copy constructor body executes, these members have already been default constructed. Knowing that these members are automatically default constructed, we can use the assignment operator to copy them:

```
TextBox::TextBox(TextBox &source) {     // definition of copy constructor
    // 1: At this point all members that are class instances have been default
    //    constructed. We now finish the copy construction process by
    //    assigning them.

    // 2: chain to base class assignment operator
    Rect::operator=(source);

    // 3: chain to data members' assignment operator
    frameThickness = source.frameThickness;
    textColor = source.textColor;

    // 4: manage memory and assign elements, note no old memory to free
    if (source.text != 0) {
        text = new char[strlen(source.text)+1];
        strcpy(text, source.text);
    }
    else {
        text = 0;
    }
}
```

Yes, there are *three* TextBoxs on the first line of the definition. TextBox is the class of this function, the name of this function, and the parameter type of this function. It is instructive to compare this definition with our definitions of the default constructor and the assignment operator in previous sections. Like the default constructor, members that are class instances are automatically default constructed. Like the assignment operator, we copy the object by assigning its members. Note that we do not need to delete[] an old value of text before allocating space for a new one, because we are creating a new object. See the previous section, which discusses the assignment operator, or see Chapter 5, if you have forgotten the meaning of the qualified syntax Rect::operator=(source).

The copy constructor is a complex function; so let's repeat the essential points. The copy constructor is invoked when an object is declared and initialized with an object of its type at the same time. We implemented the copy constructor using the member functions that implement the default constructor and the assignment operator. Class members that are instances of classes are automatically default constructed before the body of the copy constructor executes. We then explicitly chain to the assignment operator of each class member.

Implicit Copy Constructor

If you do not declare a copy constructor for a class, the class contains an implicit one. The implicit copy constructor simply chains to the copy constructor of each class member. Instances of built-in types copy construct by copying the bits from the source to the destination.

Efficient Copy Constructor with Member Initialization Lists

 We said the copy constructor was invented to prevent having to follow a default construction directly by an assignment. But we implemented the copy constructor just this way: we let the class members be default constructed and then assign to them. Why? To keep it as simple as possible. The copy constructor is complex enough without optimization issues.

It's possible to make your own copy constructor chain to the copy constructor, rather than the default constructor, of all of its members, rather than just the ones that are class instances. This involves an advanced topic called *member initialization lists*. A member initialization list is used with any constructor to tell how the class' members should be constructed. So, we might have:

```
TextBox::TextBox(TextBox &source)        // member initialization list:
    : Rect(source),                      // base class
      textColor(source.textColor),       // data member
      frameThickness(source.frameThickness), // data member
{
    if (source.text != 0) {
        text = new char[strlen(source.text)+1];
        strcpy(text, source.text);
    }
    else {
        text = 0;
    }
}
```

The list follows the function head and a colon, but precedes the function body. It tells the compiler to invoke the copy constructor for certain class members. The only work left for the copy constructor body is the relatively long code handling the `text` data member.

Classes without pointer members can often use the implicit copy constructor. For example, our `Rect` class can use its implicit version:

```
class Rect {    // can use implicit copy constructor
    // ...
private:
    int left, top;
    int width, height;
};
```

As with any member function, if you declare a copy constructor, you must define it, or you will get a linker error when you invoke it.

Note the difference in chaining behavior between the implicit and the explicit copy constructor. The implicit copy constructor chains to the *copy* constructor of *every* class member. The explicit copy constructor chains to the *default* constructor of *only* the class members that are class instances. Yes, this is confusing. It takes a while to understand the copy constructor.

Preventing Implicit Default Constructor

If you override the implicit copy constructor, you also have to override the implicit default constructor too because the compiler will not supply an implicit default constructor for you. Here's a class Foo with a copy constructor but no default constructor:

```
class Foo {
public:
    Foo(Foo &source); // overriding implicit copy constructor only
};

main() {
    Foo f;              // error: Foo does not have a default constructor
    // ...
}
```

When we try to create a Foo instance, the compiler will tell us that it doesn't have a default constructor to create it with. This error ensures that you don't accidentally forget to override the implicit default constructor. Few classes need a special copy constructor but not a special default constructor. Note that you *can* override default constructor and still use the implicit copy constructor.

Passing Objects by Value

We said a copy constructor is invoked when an object is initialized based on another object of the same type. The example of initialization we showed was an object being declared and "assigned" at the same time. Similarly, when we pass any parameter by value, we are also constructing one object based on another. For instance, here we have declared a function draw() that takes a TextBox parameter passed by value:

```
void draw(TextBox tbox);
main() {
    TextBox my_tbox;
    // ...
    draw(my_tbox);
}
```

When this function is invoked in `main()`, the parameter `tbox` is initialized based on the argument `my_tbox`. This initialization uses the copy constructor. The function `draw()` has its own copy of the `TextBox`. Any changes it makes to `tbox` will not be reflected in `my_tbox`. This is proper behavior for value parameters. So the copy constructor allows us to pass objects by value as easily as we pass instances of built-in types.

Note that the object's copy constructor is called only when we pass it by value. Here we pass a `TextBox` in three different ways:

```
void vfunc(TextBox t);  // receives object by value
void rfunc(TextBox &t); // receives object by reference
void pfunc(TextBox *t); // receives object by pointer
main() {
    TextBox tbox;
    vfunc(tbox);  // TextBox copy constructor is invoked
    rfunc(tbox);  // TextBox copy constructor is not invoked
    pfunc(&tbox); // TextBox copy constructor is not invoked
}
```

Only the call to `vfunc()` results in an invocation of `TextBox`'s copy constructor. So `vfunc()` has its own object and can do with it whatever it likes. The other two functions do not create new `TextBox` objects. Any changes they make will be reflected in the original object.

This brings us to a confusing point about copy constructors. The copy constructor takes a *reference* to an object. It is invoked, however, when an object is passed by *value*. So one of the uses of reference parameters is to enable passing class instances as value parameters.

If you forget that the parameter to a copy constructor must be a reference, you will see a C++ quirk. As we said, the copy constructor is invoked when parameters are passed by value. But, if you accidentally drop the ampersand on your copy constructor, this function itself takes a value parameter:

```
class TextBox {
public:
    TextBox(TextBox &source); // correct: takes reference parameter
    TextBox(TextBox source);  // wrong: does not take value parameter
    //...
};
```

The incorrect copy constructor invokes itself to construct its own parameter, quickly causing a stack overflow. Many compilers catch this problem.

Returning Objects by Value

A copy constructor is also used when a function result is returned by value. For example, here's a function that returns an instance of class TextBox:

```
TextBox makeTbox() {
    TextBox tbox;
    // ...
    return tbox;
}
```

In this example, tbox is used as the source to copy construct a temporary that holds the function's result. This must be done because tbox ceases to exist when the function returns, but the function value is needed by the caller. Here's a call that uses function makeTbox() (assume print() is a member function of TextBox):

```
makeTbox().print();
```

When the line above executes, here is the sequence of events:

- makeTbox() executes, invoking the TextBox default constructor to make tbox.

- makeTbox() returns tbox, invoking the TextBox copy constructor to make a copy.

- The TextBox member function print() is called on the copy just generated.

Preventing Copying

Before we finish discussing the copy constructor, we'll tell you how to turn it, and the assignment operator, off. For classes that implement basic abstractions—a rational number, a point, a time value—copying is common and important to the user. Each of these classes needs a correctly defined assignment operator and copy constructor to be a useful and complete implementation.

But you may create classes whose instances you do not want to be copied. Often this is because copying is so rare that you do not feel like defining its meaning precisely or implementing it. What should be the result of assigning one filesystem instance to another or passing a flight simulator object by value?

For classes you don't wish copied, you needn't supply an assignment operator or a copy constructor. But if you don't supply your own, you have seen that the class will contain implicit versions. These versions will certainly not do what you want. What you really want is to tell the compiler to disallow assignment and copy construction entirely.

There is a simple way to prevent assignment and copy construction. You just declare these member functions to be private and not supply definitions. Here we prevent copying of a hash table:

```
class HashTable {
public:
    void insert(char *key, int value);
    // ...

private:
    void operator=(HashTable &src);      // never defined
    HashTable(HashTable &src);           // never defined
};
```

The assignment operator and copy constructor above are private. Comments explain that the function bodies are not defined. Making them private prevents users from copying HashTables like this:

```
main() {
    HashTable h1;           // fine: invokes default constructor
    HashTable h2 = h1;      // access violation: copy constructor is private
    h2 = h1;                // access violation: assignment operator is private
}
```

The last two lines of main() cause access violations when we try to copy h1. Leaving the bodies of the private assignment operator and copy constructor is not only easier than supplying unused definitions, it causes a linker error if you accidentally try to invoke one of these functions inside a HashTable member function (where the function being private does not matter).

Printing an Object

The third member function of this chapter allows class instances to print themselves. In Chapter 2, *C++ Without Classes*, we showed you how to use C++'s *iostream* library to print instances of built-in types. Recall that we can write this:

```
#include <iostream.h>
main () {
    cout << "recall printing: " << 2 << '+' << 2 << " = " << 2+2 << '\n';
}
```

and get this on standard out:

```
recall printing: 2+2 = 4
```

Now it's time to learn how to print your own classes like this. Providing your own member function to print an object is not required, but it simplifies debugging if every class instance is able to print itself. You'll actually need to define two functions. A printing member function—called `print()`—to do the actual printing and a non-member printing operator function—called `operator<<()`—to make the invocations look like the example above. We cover these functions in the next two sections. The third section shows how to use chaining to print instances of complex classes.

The Printing Member Function

To make a class able to print itself, first add a `print()` member function:

```
class Rect {
public:
    void print(ostream *os);
    // ...
};
```

This is the function responsible for printing a `Rect` instance. The parameter to `print()` is a pointer to the `ostream` to which to print. The class `ostream` is used for output by the *iostream* library. We can, for example, pass a pointer to `cout` to this function. We might define the `print()` function like this:

```
void Rect::print(ostream *os) {
    *os << "Rect{" << top << ", " << left << ", "
        << width << ", " << height << "}";
}
```

This prints the class of the object and its four data members. We can now print out `Rect` objects like this:

```
#include <iostream.h>
main() {
    Rect r;
    // ...
    cout << "the rect is: "
    r.print(&cout);          // prints r to cout
    cout << '\n';
}
```

We might get something like this:

```
the rect is: Rect{1, 2, 3, 4}
```

The Printing Operator

To use the printing operator to print your own classes, you define a nonmember function:

```
ostream &operator<<(ostream &os, Rect &r) {
    r.print(&os);
    return os;
}
```

This global function, named `operator<<`, makes printing a `Rect` easy. It takes a reference to the `ostream` to print to and a reference to the `Rect` to print. It calls the `print()` member function for the `Rect` and returns a reference to the `ostream` it printed to.

Note that `operator<<()` is a global function rather than a member function like `operator=()` would be. Each class has its own global `operator<<()`. These `operator<<()` functions are distinguished from the each other by their second parameters (the type of the object to print). This is another example of function overloading.[*]

Now we can print `Rects` as easily as any built-in type:

```
main() {
    Rect r;
    // ...
    cout << "the rect is: "
    cout << r;              // prints r to cout
    cout << '\n';
}
```

The compiler translates the expression `cout << r` into the invocation:

```
operator<<(cout, r);        // compiler's translation of "cout << r"
```

We can actually write:

```
cout << "the rect is: " << r << '\n';
```

which translates to:

```
operator<<(operator<<(operator<<(cout, "the rect is: "), r), '\n');
```

Reading from the inside out, we see three invocations of the overloaded `operator<<()` function. This shows why our `operator<<(ostream &, Rect &)` returned a reference to the `ostream` it printed to. This reference becomes the `ostream` parameter to the next `operator<<()` call. This allows us to use our `Rect` as part of a chain of printing.

Note that we used references for `operator<<(ostream &, Rect &)` but a pointer for `Rect::print(ostream *)`. We could have used a reference in our `print()` function. But we prefer to stick with pointers, unless necessary, because they are less confusing than references for the beginner. (See Chapter 8, for a refresher on reference if needed.)

---

[*] Why is `operator=()` a member function while `operator<<()` is a global function? Basically, we cannot make our `operator<<()` a member function because we want to write `cout << my_object` with the object we are printing second rather than first. If a binary operator like `=` or `<<` is going to be a member function, it must be a member of the class it takes on its left-hand side.

Chaining Printing Member Functions

The compiler helps us with most of the member functions discussed in this chapter and in Chapter 6. For example, a class contains an implicit default constructor if we do not supply one. Even when we do supply our own default constructor, the compiler helps by automatically chaining our default constructor to the appropriate default constructors in that class' members. We get no such help with the print() member function. In this section we discuss how to print a large class using the printing capabilities of its members.

For example, now that we can print a Rect, we can use this to help us print a TextBox. Recall that the definition of a TextBox is:

```
class TextBox : public Rect {     // recall this class definition from
    // ...                         // the beginning of the chapter
private:
    Color textColor;
    int frameThickness;
    char *text;
};
```

TextBox is derived from Rect and has three data members: a Color, an int, and a char*. The *iostream* library comes able to print int and char* instances. We extended it in the previous two sections to make it able to print a Rect instance. Once we similarly add the ability to print a Color instance, the following code makes a TextBox print itself:

```
void TextBox::print(ostream *os) {
    *os << "TextBox{";
    Rect::print(os);
    *os << ", " << textColor << ", " << frameThickness << ", "
        << '"' << text << '"' << "}";
}
```

We use the printing operator to print each data member. For the base class Rect, however, we use a qualified call to Rect::print(). This is because TextBox cannot print its base part with a call to *os << *this or simply print(os); these will print out the entire TextBox recursively. We could have called cout << *(Rect *)this to print the base class, but casting should only be used when necessary. Avoiding casts becomes even more important when we cover polymorphism in Chapter 12, *Polymorphism with Virtual Functions*. Instead, the qualified call to Rect::print() invokes the correct function to print the base class without a cast.

Now all we need is the nonmember function:

```
ostream &operator<<(ostream &os, TextBox &tbox) {
    tbox.print(&os);
    return os;
}
```

This function takes a reference to the ostream to print to and a reference to the TextBox to print. It calls the print() member function for the TextBox and returns a reference to the ostream it printed to. We can now print a TextBox object:

```
main() {
    TextBox tbox;
    // ...
    cout << "the text box is: " << tbox << '\n';
}
```

and get something like this:

```
the text box is: TextBox{Rect{10, 30, 94, 12}, Color{1023}, 8, "Hello?"}
```

There is nothing special about the convention we have chosen to display the class instance. You do not need to show the class name or enclose the class data in braces like we have. We find this convention useful, but you may choose a more compact or more verbose method.

Unlike the other functions introduced in these two chapters, the printing functions do not have a special relationship with the compiler. All of the printing is handled by the *iostream* library. Even the printing of built-in types is implemented as standard function calls. That even type-safe, extensible I/O can be implemented at the user level shows some of the power of C++.

Summary

Before we end this chapter, we present a class with declarations for all the special member functions (and the important global function) we cover in this book:

```
class TextBox {                         // special member functions:
public:
    TextBox();                              // default constructor
    ~TextBox();                             // destructor
    void operator=(TextBox &source);        // assignment operator
    TextBox(TextBox &source);               // copy constructor
    void print(ostream *os);                // printing member function
    // ...
};

                                        // important global function:
ostream &operator<<(ostream &os, TextBox &tb); // printing operator
```

10

An Example Class

You've now seen all the special member functions that every class uses. It's time to tie it all together with a realistic example. In this chapter we'll study a single abstraction through a few different implementations. We'll focus on the special member functions needed by each successive implementation. This should help you understand the purpose, usefulness, and power of these member functions.

The abstraction we'll implement represents an identification number, like a part number used in factories. It is useful to wrap this simple concept in a class, even if at first you think it can be implemented as an integer. Later you may need a larger range of values. If you've abstracted well, you can easily accommodate this design change.

The class implementing our abstraction has the following interface, which will not change:

```
class Id {
public:
    Id();                    // default constructor
    ~Id();                   // destructor
    void operator=(Id &src); // assignment operator
    Id(Id &src);             // copy constructor

public:
    void print(ostream *os); // printing mem func (we'll also use operator<<())
    void set(char *idStr);   // sets value

private:
    // data will evolve
};
```

The class is called `Id`. It needs a default constructor, a destructor, an assignment operator, and a copy constructor. Depending on the implementation, the implicit versions of these member functions may be adequate. In that case, we must not declare the ones we want the compiler to use the implicit versions of. The only other things we can do with our Id class is print() it out and set() its value. Note that set() takes a char*. This will be a null-terminated string holding a value representing the Id.

To make an Id truly useful, we need to compare Id instances, so we can order them for searching. We might even want to hash Id instances, enabling us to store them in a hash table. You can easily implement these member functions given a fixed implementation of Id's data. Because we want to focus on the special member functions, we won't spend time on these useful, but simple, other functions.

We have not shown what data the Id class has, because we vary the data. First, we'll implement an Id as a simple int, then as a static array, then as a dynamic array. Finally, we'll optimize this dynamic-array representation to avoid lots of copying. Once you've seen us evolve this class, you'll be ready to learn some more about the special member functions. The last two sections of this chapter present some advanced information on the special member functions, focusing most on the copy constructor.

Using an int

The simplest implementation of Id uses a single int. Here is what the class definition looks like in this case:

```
class Id {     // implemented as an int
public:
    Id();
    // uses implicit ~Id();
    // uses implicit void operator=(Id &src);
    // uses implicit Id(Id &src);

public:
    void print(ostream *os);
    void set(char *idStr);

private:
    int value;
};
```

The only data member is an int called value. With an int data member, we can use the implicit versions of some of the member functions. We can use the implicit destructor, because an Id instance has no resources we need to free. We can also use the implicit assignment operator and copy constructor because an int copies correctly automatically.

A class' implicit default constructor does not automatically chain to anything that will put an int data member like value into a valid default state. So we need to create an explicit default constructor. Here is a version that just sets value to zero, a reasonable default:

```
Id::Id() {
    value = 0;
}
```

Printing out an Id instance is not much more complex than creating one. Here is an implementation of print() and its associate operator<<():

```
void Id::print(ostream *os) {
    *os << "Id{" << value << '}';
}

ostream &operator<<(ostream &os, Id &theId) {
    theId.print(&os);
    return os;
}
```

The printing member function print() shows the class and the value of the data member value. The printing operator operator<<() simply calls the printing member function on the Id instance passed and then returns the ostream instance it printed to.

The last member function we need for our int implementation of Id is the member function to set() the value of an Id instance:

```
void Id::set(char *idStr) {
    if (idStr == 0)
        error("bad id");
    value = atoi(idStr);
}
```

This member function converts the string passed in idStr into an int using the standard function atoi(). The only error checking shown ensures that the string passed is not null. A robust implementation would also check that the string contains only valid digits and represents a number in the range of int. We leave this out for brevity. If an error is found, we call our own error handling routine error(), which terminates the program with a message.

We've finished our first implementation of Id. Here is a short program using it:

```
#include <stdlib.h>    // to get atoi() and exit()
#include <string.h>    // to get strcpy() and strlen() (needed later)
#include <limits.h>    // to get UINT_MAX (needed later)
#include <iostream.h>  // to get new-style output
#include "id.h"        // to get Id class

void error(char *msg) {
```

```
        cerr << "error: " << msg << '\n';
        exit(1);
}

main() {
    Id id1;                             // tests default constructor
    Id id2 = id1;                       // tests copy constructor
    cout << "id1 = " << id1 << '\n';   // tests operator<<() and print()
    cout << "id2 = " << id2 << '\n';

    id1.set("12345");                   // tests set()
    cout << "id1 = " << id1 << '\n';

    id2 = id1;                          // tests assignment operator
    cout << "id2 = " << id2 << '\n';

}                                       // tests destructor
```

This program #includes all the headers we'll need in this and the following sections. It creates two Id instances, id1 and id2. The comments show what member functions a given line exercises. When run, this program prints:

```
id1 = Id{0}
id2 = Id{0}
id1 = Id{12345}
id2 = Id{12345}
```

Using a Static Array

Now, say we've released our Id class into the world, and the program requirements change. Instead of being a number, an Id is actually a string of arbitrary text characters, up to a maximum of sixteen characters. If we previously implemented an Id as a typedef of an int, this change might require changing a lot of code that uses Id. But, because we abstracted the type with a class, we can just change the implementation. No Id user needs to know that anything has changed, except that the string passed to set() can now contain any character, not just digits.

Here is the definition of our new Id class:

```
#define MAX_ID_LEN 16

class Id {    // implemented as a static array
public:
    Id();
    // uses implicit ~Id();
    // uses implicit void operator=(Id &src);
    // uses implicit Id(Id &src);

public:
    void print(ostream *os);
    void set(char *idStr);
```

```
private:
    char value[MAX_ID_LEN+1];
};
```

This time the single data member `value` is a static array of `char`s. It is large enough to hold a string of up to `MAX_ID_LEN` characters, with one character for the null terminator. As in the previous section, the implicit destructor works for this implementation, because this class has no resources you need to free. Also, an `Id` instance assigns and copy constructs correctly automatically. This is because `value` is not a pointer, but an array completely contained in the class; so the compiler copies the characters correctly.

We must, however, override the implicit default constructor to set the contents of `value`. We'll make it behave as the `int`-based `Id` did, setting the instance to have a value of zero:

```
Id::Id() {
    value[0] = '0';
    value[1] = '\0';
}
```

In this implementation, an `Id` of zero is created by storing the single character `'0'` followed by the null terminator.

We do not need to change the implementation of the `print()` member function from the version we showed in the previous section. Moreover, because the printing operator `operator<<()` calls only the `print()` member function on an `Id` instance, we'll never need to change its implementation as long as we maintain the interface to `Id`. So we can skip both of these functions.

The only other function we need to change is `set()`:

```
void Id::set(char *idStr) {
    if (idStr == 0 || strlen(idStr) > MAX_ID_LEN)
        error("bad id");
    strcpy(value, idStr);
}
```

If there is no problem, the `idStr` is simply copied into the `value` data member using `strcpy()`. We can now run the previous program to test this new implementation of `Id`.

Using a Dynamic Array

The previous two examples both benefited from three implicit member functions handled by the compiler. If our requirements change to say that an `Id` can be a string of any length, we aren't so lucky. In this case, the class definition looks like this:

```
class Id {     // implemented as a dynamic array
public:
    Id();
    ~Id();
    void operator=(Id &src);
    Id(Id &src);

public:
    void print(ostream *os);
    void set(char *idStr);

private:
    void newVal(char *val);
    void deleteVal();

private:
    char *value;
};
```

This time we have declared all the special member functions, because none of the implicit versions will do.[*] The implicit versions are inadequate because the single data member `value` is now a `char*`. This data member enables an `Id` instance to hold a string of any length. But, as we stressed in Chapter 6, *Better Abstraction with Constructors and Destructors*, and Chapter 9, *Better Abstraction with Other Special Member Functions*, pointers do not usually behave as you want in the implicit versions of the special member functions.

Note that overriding special member functions previously supplied by the compiler implicitly does not change the interface to the class as far as the `Id` user is concerned. The declarations simply say that we are supplying the definitions, rather than the compiler. The `Id` user should see no change in the behavior of the `Id` instances.

In addition to declaring all the special member functions in the `Id` class, we've declared two private member functions, `newVal()` and `deleteVal()`. These functions handle the data member `value`. The data member gets set by a call to `newVal()`; the argument to `newVal()` is the string to set `value` to:

```
void Id::newVal(char *val) {
    if (val == 0)
        error("bad id");
    value = new char[strlen(val)+1];
```

---

* Previously the implicit destructor, assignment operator, and copy constructor were all valid. Now none of the implicit versions are correct. This all-or-none situation is not unusual for these three special member functions. Typically these three functions can either all use their implicit versions, or all need explicit versions.

```
            strcpy(value, val);
    }
```

We first check that the string passed is not null. We then use `new[]` to allocate space for the string. Remember from Chapter 7, *Better Abstraction with new and delete*, that, by default, `new[]` terminates the program if it cannot allocate the memory. We use `strcpy()` to copy the string. Note that we are not freeing the contents of `value` before allocating new memory. It is assumed that you have done this before calling `newVal()`, probably by calling `deleteVal()`:

```
void Id::deleteVal() {
    delete[] value;
}
```

This simply calls the operator `delete[]` on `value`.

We have put the allocation and freeing code into their own private member functions so that we can call them from all the special member functions. Each has its own requirements for exactly what to do—some have no data to free, others do not need allocation—and these two member functions give us the flexibility we need. Here is the default constructor and the destructor:

```
Id::Id() {
    newVal("0");
}

Id::~Id() {
    deleteVal();
}
```

The default constructor simply calls `newVal()` with a string containing only zero. This keeps the default `Id` the same as in the previous two sections. The destructor only needs to call `deleteVal()` to free the string. The assignment operator and copy constructor look like this:

```
void Id::operator=(Id &src) {
    deleteVal();
    newVal(src.value);
}

Id::Id(Id &src) {
    newVal(src.value);
}
```

The assignment operator calls `deleteVal()` to destroy the previous string and `newVal()` with the new string to copy. The copy constructor only calls `newVal()`, passing the string from its parameter `src`. (In this example, the assignment operator behaves like a destructor call followed by a copy constructor call. The assignment operator often behaves like a combination of these two functions.)

In Chapter 9, we made a big deal about the steps you need to follow to make sure that the assignment operator and copy constructor chain correctly. For a complex class like our `TextBox` example, you should follow these rules. In this simple `Id` class (with only one data member and no base class), we are less formal and have not strictly followed these rules.

As in the previous section, the implementation of printing has not changed, but `set()` has changed:

```
void Id::set(char *idStr) {
    deleteVal();
    newVal(idStr);
}
```

This is very similar to the assignment operator, except that it takes a `char*` not an `Id`. We can now test this completed implementation with the same test program we used previously.

Using a Reference-Counted String

We've taken our `Id` class from a simple `int` to an unlimited string. How much more can the requirements change? Now, instead of expanding the range of what an `Id` can contain, the users are complaining that the code is too slow. The problem is that an `Id` is thought of as a simple piece of data. As a result, `Id` instances are treated like you would treat an `int`: copied often, passed by value, etc. Now that `Id`s can contain large strings, this slows down the program too much.

We could require `Id` instances to be treated with less abandon. Use pointers to `Id`s now that they are large, we might say. But, as you have seen throughout this book, pointers can be awkward and hard to use, compared to classes. They don't, in general, construct, copy, or destruct correctly. Requiring the use of a pointer, rather than a class, forces the user to keep these issues in mind. Also, if our goal is to preserve a large base of code, we don't want to make such a fundamental change. So requiring pointers is out.

Well, almost out. What we'll do is hide the pointer in our `Id` class, letting it handle the sticky issues. We'll make `Id` point to a new class, `IdData`, which will contain the real information. In addition, `IdData` will hold a reference count, telling how many `Id` instances point to a given `IdData` instance. This reference count is the key to speeding up the run-time. When we copy an `Id` instance, we can point it at the same `IdData` instance as the source of the copy and increment the reference count. When an `Id` instance is destroyed, we decrement its `IdData` instance's reference count, not destroying the `IdData` instance until the reference count reaches zero. So passing an `Id` instance by value results only in the creation of another pointer to the same piece of data and the bumping of a reference count.

To implement this new Id we take what we've been calling our Id class and make it into a class called IdData:

```
class IdData {        // identical to Id in the previous section
    friend class Id; // (except for friend decl and refCount data member)

public:
    IdData();
    ~IdData();
    void operator=(IdData &src);
    IdData(IdData &src);

public:
    void print(ostream *os);
    void set(char *idStr);

private:
    void newVal(char *val);
    void deleteVal();

private:
    char *value;
    unsigned refCount;
};
```

The class is identical to Id in the previous section, except that it now declares Id to be a friend and has a new data member called refCount. The definitions of the member functions do not change from the previous section, except the default and copy constructors must set refCount to zero and the print() member function shows the class name as IdData and the value of refCount. We aren't showing these simple changes.

The new Id now looks like this:

```
class Id {      // implemented as a reference-counted string
public:
    Id();
    ~Id();
    void operator=(Id &src);
    Id(Id &src);

public:
    void print(ostream *os);
    void set(char *idStr);

private:
    void attachData(IdData *theData);
    void detachData();

private:
    IdData *data;
};
```

It declares all the special member functions, because we'll need to provide definitions for them all. The only data member in this class, data, points to an IdData
instance. Making this data member a pointer allows us to share a single IdData
instance among multiple Id instances. Finally, instead of newVal() and deleteVal()
helper functions from the previous section, this class has attachData() and
detachData() to handle the IdData. These functions do most of the work, so we'll
implement them first:

```
void Id::attachData(IdData *theData) {
    if (theData == 0) {
        // no data to attach to, make new data
        data = new IdData;
    }
    else if (theData->refCount == UINT_MAX) {
        // avoid reference count overflow, make new data
        data = new IdData;
        set(theData->value);
    }
    else {
        // simply attach to data
        data = theData;
    }
    ++data->refCount;
}

void Id::detachData() {
    if (--data->refCount == 0)
        delete data;
}
```

The detachData() member function decrements the reference count in the IdData
instance pointed to by the data data member. If this reference count falls to zero,
this is the last Id instance pointing to this IdData instance, and the IdData instance
is freed.

The attachData() member function is a bit more complicated. If passed the null
pointer, it creates a new IdData instance to point to. If passed something other
than the null pointer, it points right at that IdData instance. In the rare case when
the reference count overflows, we must create a new IdData instance to hold the
copied data. Note that the old value of data is not freed in attachData(); this must
be done before calling attachData(). Once data is set to the correct value, the reference count on the IdData instance is incremented.

Now, as in the previous section, most of the special member functions can be
implemented in terms of these two helper functions:

```
Id::Id() {
    attachData(0);
}
```

```
Id::~Id() {
    detachData();
}

void Id::operator=(Id &src) {
    detachData();
    attachData(src.data);
}

Id::Id(Id &src) {
    attachData(src.data);
}
```

The default constructor calls `attachData()` with the null pointer, to create a new `IdData` instance to point at. The destructor calls `detachData()` to signal that this `Id` instance no longer points at this data. The assignment operator detaches from its old data and attaches to the new data. The copy constructor attaches to new data without detaching from any old data.

The printing member function now looks like this:

```
void Id::print(ostream *os) {
    *os << "Id{" << data << "-->";
    if (data == 0)
        *os << "(null)";
    else
        *os << *data;
    *os << '}';
}
```

It shows the value of the `data` pointer and what that data member points to if it is not null. The printing operator `operator<<()` is identical to what you've seen in the previous sections.

The final member function left to define is `set()`:

```
void Id::set(char *idStr) {
    if (data->refCount > 1)
        attachData(0);
    data->set(idStr);
}
```

First we make sure that the `Id` instance is pointing to its own copy of the `IdData` instance. Then we call `set()` on `data` to change the value of this `IdData` instance. The class is now complete. Running the test program produces something like the following output (your pointer values might be different):

```
id1 = Id{0x22640-->IdData{0, refCount = 2}}
id2 = Id{0x22660-->IdData{0, refCount = 2}}
id1 = Id{0x22640-->IdData{12345, refCount = 1}}
id2 = Id{0x22640-->IdData{12345, refCount = 2}}
```

Copy Constructor Quiz

To help you better understand the hardest special member function, the copy constructor, this section has a brief quiz. Trying to answer each question should force you to clarify the role of the copy constructor in C++. The answers follow the questions, but try to answer each one yourself first. Review Chapter 8, *References*, and Chapter 9, if you don't understand something.

All questions involve these four functions:

```
Id  func_vv(Id param)   {return param;}
Id  func_rv(Id &param)  {return param;}
Id &func_vr(Id param)   {return param;}
Id &func_rr(Id &param)  {return param;}
```

Here, func_vv() takes an Id by value and returns one by value; func_rv() takes a reference parameter and returns by value; func_vr() has a value parameter and a reference return; and func_rr() takes and returns by reference. Each function simply returns its parameter.

Question 1: *Which of the four functions shown above returns bad data?*

Answer 1: The function func_vr() returns bad data. You should not return a local variable (in this case the value parameter) by reference. The reference is bound to an object that no longer exists.

Question 2: *Of the three legal functions, which of these cannot take its own result as a parameter? In other words, which of these calls is illegal?*

```
main() {
    Id id0;
    func_vv(func_vv(id0));
    func_rv(func_rv(id0));
    func_rr(func_rr(id0));
}
```

Answer 2: The second call is illegal. The function func_rv() cannot take its own result as a parameter. The compiler will not bind a reference parameter to a temporary, like the one generated by a value return.

Question 3: *How many copy constructor calls does each line of* main() *below generate (assuming the compiler does not optimize any away, which it might)?*

```
main() {
    Id id0;
    func_vv(id0);
    func_rv(id0);
    func_rr(id0);
}
```

Answer 3: The declaration of id0 causes no copy constructor calls (only a default constructor call); the call to func_vv() causes two (one for the value parameter, one for the value return); the call to func_rv() causes one (to create the value return); the call to func_rr() causes no copy constructor calls.

Question 4: *How many copy constructor calls does each line of* main() *below cause (assuming no optimizations)?*

```
main() {
    Id id0;
    Id id1 = func_rr(id0);
    id1 = func_vv(func_rv(func_rr(id0)));
    id1 = func_vv(func_vv(func_vv(id0)));
    id1 = func_rr(func_rr(func_rr(func_rr(id0))));
}
```

Answer 4: Again, the first line of main() invokes only the default constructor; the second line invokes the copy constructor one time (to create id1); the third line invokes the copy constructor three times (for the value return from func_rv() and the value parameter and value return from func_vv()); the fourth line invokes the copy constructor six times (twice for each value parameter and return in func_vv()); the fifth line does not invoke the copy constructor at all.

Summary Table

The next page contains a table that tries to summarize all the important aspects of the special member functions we've covered in this book.

Name	Declaration (for class Id)	Purpose	Behavior of Implicit Version	Automatic Chaining in Explicit Version	When Invoked (besides chaining)
Default constructor	Id()	Create object from scratch	Chains to default constructor of class members that are class instances	Chains to default constructor of class members that are class instances before executing function body	When object is created from scratch (e.g., control passes over local declaration or new is called)
Destructor	~Id()	Clean up after object	Chains to destructor of class members that are class instances	Chains to destructor of class members that are class instances after executing function body	When object is done being used (e.g., scope of local is exited or delete called)
Assignment operator	void operator= (Id &src)	Assign to object	Chains to assignment operator of all class members	No automatic chaining in explicit version	By assignment (a=b) or explicit invocation (a.operator=(b))
Copy constructor	Id(Id &src)	Create object based on another object	Chains to copy constructor of all class members	Chains to default constructor of class members that are class instances before executing function body	When object is created based on another of the same type (e.g., by a declaration and initialization, pass-by-value, or return-by-value)
Printing member function	void print (ostream *os)	Print object	No implicit version (but is inherited)	No automatic chaining in explicit version	Only when explicitly called[a]

a. Usually by the printing operator: ostream &operator<<(ostream &os, Id &i).

Table 10-1: Summary of Special Member Functions

11

Better Hierarchy with Templates

A template is a definition of a class with parts of it parameterized. For example, instead of writing a separate definition for each kind of array (e.g., `IntArray`, `DoubleArray`, etc.), we can define a template `Array` that expands into an array of any type: `Array<int>`, `Array<double>`, etc. One definition gets us all the different arrays we want.

In C we can write code that manipulates an array of any type, using casts to and from `void*`. We can use casts in C++ too, of course, but that is not type-safe. Using templates to manipulate an array of any type allows flexibility without sacrificing type safety. So templates allow a more powerful kind of hierarchy.

In the next two sections of this chapter we show how to define a template, then how to use the template to define objects. In the last two sections we discuss two problems you can run into with templates.

Defining a Template

Let's return to our `IntArray` class and parameterize the type of the elements. Here's the class definition from the original example:

```
class IntArray {
public:
    IntArray();
    ~IntArray();
    void    setSize(size_t value);
    size_t  getSize();
    void    setElem(size_t index, int value);
    int     getElem(size_t index);

private:
    int *elems;
```

```
        size_t numElems;
    };
```

Now let's make it an array of anything:

```
    template<class Type>              // "Type" is the abstracted type
    class Array {                     // "IntArray" changed to "Array"
    public:
        Array();                      // "IntArray" changed to "Array"
        ~Array();                     // "IntArray" changed to "Array"
        void    setSize(size_t value);
        size_t  getSize();
        void    setElem(size_t index, Type value);   // "int" changed to "Type"
        Type    getElem(size_t index);               // "int" changed to "Type"

    private:
        Type *elems;                  // "int" changed to "Type"
        size_t numElems;
    };
```

In the first line, `template` is a keyword introducing the template. Following this, enclosed in angle brackets, is the parameter taken by the template. The keyword `class` says that the parameter can be any type, including a built-in type. `Type` is the name we have chosen for our parameter.

We changed the name of the class from `IntArray` to `Array` because it is no longer limited to `int`s. `Array` is not a class, but a template for creating a whole family of array classes that differ only by element type. The only other changes from the `IntArray` class to the `Array` template are where we replaced `int` with `Type` everywhere `int` was used: as the type of a parameter to `setElem()`, the return type of `getElem()`, and the type of data member `elems`.

We've converted the class definition into a class template. Now we must convert all the member functions as well. We'll show you how to convert the constructor, `setElem()`, `getElem()`, and `setSize()` into member function templates. There are no changes in the bodies of the first three member functions because they don't refer to `int`, so we aren't showing them. We'll show and discuss each of the remaining member function in turn. First here's the constructor before and after turning it into a template:

```
    IntArray::IntArray() {  // before turning into template
        // ...
    }

    template<class Type>    // after turning into template
    Array<Type>::Array() {
        // ...
    }
```

You must repeat the `template` statement for every member function, as we show above. We recommend that you name the parameter what you used with the original template definition (in this case, `Type`), although the language doesn't require it.

When you specify the class name with the scope operator (`::`), you must include the `<Type>`, which is part of the class name. But with the constructor you don't include the `<Type>` with the function name. So it's `Array<Type>::Array()` rather than `Array<Type>::Array<Type>()`, as you might guess at first. The reason is that `Array<Type>` is the class name, and `Array` is the function name. You must use the class name before the `::`, and the function name after. Now here's `setElem()` before and after conversion into a template:

```
void IntArray::setElem(size_t index, int value) {      // before template
    // ...
}

template<class Type>                                    // after template
void Array<Type>::setElem(size_t index, Type value) {
    // ...
}
```

For `setElem()` we again see the repeated `template` statement, and the `Array<Type>::`. We also see that the type for the parameter `value` is `Type`, matching the function's declaration. Now here's `getElem()` before and after:

```
int IntArray::getElem(size_t index) {      // before template
    // ...
}

template<class Type>                        // after template
Type Array<Type>::getElem(size t index) {
    // ...
}
```

Again note the repeated `template` statement, and the `Array<Type>::`. Here the type of the return is `Type`, matching the function's declaration. Finally, here's `setSize()` before and after:

```
void IntArray::setSize(unsigned value) {     // before template
    delete[] elems;
    numElems = value;
    elems = new int[value];
}

template<class Type>                          // after template
void Array<Type>::setSize(unsigned value) {
    delete[] elems;
    numElems = value;
    elems = new Type[value];
}
```

And yet again note the repeated `template` statement and the `Array<Type>::`. The new point to note in `setSize()` is that there is a use of `Type`, within the body of the function, with the `new[]` operator. Anywhere in the body of the functions that you refer to the type, you replace the explicit type with the type identifier specified in our `template` statement, which is `Type` here.

Using a Template to Define an Object

Now that we have defined a template, we can use it to define an object. Here's an example of using a template:

```
Array<int> ia;        // IntArray replaced with Array<int>
unsigned n;
int x;
// ...
ia.setElem(n, x);
// ...
x = ia.getElem(n);
```

The code looks the same as using our original `IntArray` class, except we've replaced `IntArray` with `Array<int>` in the definition of ia. `Array<int>` is a valid C++ class, and we can use it anywhere you use a C++ class name.

But what really happens when you use templates to define objects? When the compiler sees `Array<int>`, it expands template `Array`, replacing `Type` with `int`, generating the class `Array<int>`. The compiler only has to expand once for a specific type of parameter (i.e., once for `Array<int>`, once for `Array<double>`, and so on), although some compilers have trouble when we use the template in several files.

Think of templates as macro definitions expanded by the compiler instead of by a preprocessor. When a preprocessor does macro expansion, it blindly substitutes arguments. The compiler has access to more information than the preprocessor and performs much more intelligent expansion.

Now we can define an array of any type:

```
Array<double> da;              // parameter is built-in type
Array<PayPerViewChannel> pa;   // parameter is class
Array<Array<int> > iaa;        // parameter is expanded template
//                  ^ note space
```

This shows that you can use any type as the parameter `Type` in `Array<Type>`, including a built-in type, user-defined class, or expanded template. Using an expanded template as a parameter to a template is surprisingly free of surprises, except that if you fail to put in a space between the two ">"s, you end up with ">>". The compiler considers that an operator and gives us an error.

But what do you get with `Array<Array<int> > iaa`? It creates an array of arrays. `iaa.getElem(3)` returns array 3 of the array of arrays, and `iaa.getElem(3).getElem(4)` returns element 4 of array 3. If you want to modify the elements you'll need to access the elements with pointers instead, because otherwise we'll be modifying copies instead of the original elements. See the last section of this chapter on modifying elements of container classes.

Careful with That Expansion, Eugene

Now that you know how to define and use a template, we need to urge you to think about what's happening when you use a template to define an object. Every function of, and operator on, a type parameter, which is `Type` in our examples above, must be defined for the type you substitute. Even more importantly, the definitions must be right. To illustrate, suppose you define a `SortedArray<Type>` class. In order to sort, you'll have a comparison somewhere in your class definition:

```
// return less than 0 if a < b, 0 if a = b, and greater than 0 if a > b
template<class Type>
int SortedArray<Type>::compare(Type a, Type b) {
    return a - b;
}
```

From the above you can see that we have a class called `SortedArray<Type>`, which presumably sorts elements of whatever type you specify when you use the template. Here we see the `compare()` function, and from the comment we know what it's supposed to return, based on the relative values of a and b. There are three possibilities: types with subtraction defined, types with it not defined, and types with it defined but not how you want.

When you use this template for built-in types, they will have subtraction defined:

```
SortedArray<int> sai;
SortedArray<double> sad;
```

The two uses of `SortedArray<Type>` are with the two built-in types, `int` and `double`. Subtraction is defined for both of those types, so the compiler knows what to do with the expression a - b in `compare()`.

Now suppose you use `SortedArray<Type>` for a class that doesn't have subtraction defined. `SortedArray<Type>`'s expansion includes code that subtracts two instances of the parameterized type, so the compiler will produce an error. That's not so bad. Now let's define a sorted array of strings:

```
SortedArray<char*> sac;
```

Here we see the template used for type `char*`. Oops! Subtraction is defined for `char*`, but not the way you want. It will compare addresses of the strings rather than comparing the strings. This is why we said it's even more important that the definitions be "right." When you create a sorted array of `char*`, the compiler doesn't complain at all, but you end up with a nasty bug to track down. This is why you must think about what's happening when you use a template.

Here's how to fix the `char*` problem, once you've tracked it down. You override the compare member function of the template with an explicit definition of `compare(char*,char*)`:

```
int SortedArray<char*>::compare(char *a, char *b) {
    return strcmp(a, b);
}
```

When the compiler needs `SortedArray<char*>`, it uses this definition of compare instead of expanding it from the template. This definition is called a *specialization* because you are creating a special definition for the compiler to use instead of expanding the generic one. Make sure the return type and all the parameter types match exactly in order for the compiler to detect your specialization. This is different from overloading, where the return type is irrelevant.

It's a good idea to include the requirements on operators in your documentation of your template. This will help other users of the template avoid the problem above and remind you, too.

Modifying Container Class Elements

There's one more problem we want to warn you about when you use templates. It has to do with modifying elements of container classes outside the class. A container class is a class that contains a collection of elements, like an array or tree. We recommend using templates for type-safe container classes; that's why we describe this in the template chapter.

To show the problem we need two things: a container class using a template and a type that has a function that modifies instances of itself. Here we have a definition of such a container class and type, along with an expansion of the template for the type:

```
// a template defining an array
template<class T>
class Array {
    // a member function returning element n of the array
    T getElem(int n);
    // ...
};
```

Other Kinds of Templates and Template Parameters

 Templates can expand into things other than classes; they can expand into functions, for instance, and even into other templates. Function templates are useful for replacing parameterized macros, which can be unsafe due to problems like using ++ on a parameter. Here's a replacement for the classic `max` macro:

```
template<class ParamType>
ParamType max(ParamType p1, ParamType p2) {return p1 > p2 ? p1 : p2;}
```

In this example, `max` is a function template that returns the maximum of its parameters. Function templates can get complicated because it is not always clear when a function invocation matches a function template.

Templates can also take fancier parameters. They can take more than one, for instance. And a parameter does not have to represent an unknown type: a template can take a number; so, for example, you could define a static array of length `NumElems` using a template with integer parameter `NumElems`:

```
template<class ElemType, int NumElems>
class StaticArray{/*...*/}
```

The second parameter here must be an integer. The keyword `class` is used when parameters can be any type. Specific types, like `int` in the example above, are used to restrict the type of a parameter.

```
// a user-defined type MyType
class MyType {
public:
    // a member function that modifies instances of MyType
    void sanitize();
    // ...
};

// ...
// an array of elements of type MyType
Array<MyType> anArray;
```

Above we have a template `Array<T>`, a user-defined class `MyType`, and an array `anArray` that uses the template to make an array of elements of type `MyType`. The template has a member function `getElem()` that returns an element of the array. `MyType` has a member function `sanitize()` that modifies instances of itself.

Now suppose you want to modify element five of the array, using `sanitize()`. The first thing you might try is:

```
anArray.getElem(5).sanitize();    // WRONG: modifies copy of element five
```

Here we see `anArray`, which is an instance of the `Array` class, `getElem(5)`, which returns the fifth element of the array, and `sanitize()`, which modifies it. But `getElem()` returns a copy of element five, so you'll sanitize a *copy* of element five of the array, not the element itself. OOP and C++ conspire to trick you into making this mistake, which is difficult to catch. One solution is to provide a member function that returns a pointer to the element in the `Array` template. In the following example we add `getElemPtr()` to return the pointer:

```
template<class T>
class Array {
    T getElem(int n);
    T *getElemPtr(int n);  // new function
    // ...
};
// ...
anArray.getElemPtr(5)->sanitize();
```

Here we've added another member function, `getElemPtr()`, to the template. Instead of returning a copy of the element, as `getElem()` does, it returns a pointer to the element. We've also changed `anArray.getElem(5).sanitize` to `anArray.getElemPtr(5)->sanitize()`, so now `sanitize()` acts on the original element in the array, rather than a copy of it.

12

Polymorphism with Virtual Functions

> *You are about to enter another dimension.*
> *A dimension not of static but of dynamic typing.*
> *You are about to enter the polymorphism zone.*
>
> —Rod Stroustrup.

If Stroustrup had stopped with only the topics we have explained so far, C++ would be a complete language. Languages containing only the abstraction, encapsulation, and hierarchy features we have seen are called object-*based* languages. To qualify as object-oriented, a language also needs to support polymorphism.

Polymorphism allows us to use different objects in the same code. As we said in Chapter 1, *Object-Oriented Programming with Classes*, the classic example is a group of classes representing different shapes, like triangles, polygons, etc. Shapes share abilities: they can all draw themselves, they can all return their perimeter, etc. The implementation of each ability, however, changes with each shape. For example, we calculate the area of a triangle and a circle using different equations. With polymorphism, we can write code in terms of a generic shape and make the code work correctly for any actual shape.

This generic shape is polymorphic—literally *many forms*—because at any particular point during program execution it can be a rectangle, an oval, etc. Polymorphism requires the generic shape to behave differently at run-time depending on the *actual* type of shape it is. This dynamic-typing nature of polymorphism is difficult to mesh with the static-typing nature of C. That is why we must spend a good deal of time explaining how polymorphism works in C++.

First, we'll see how C programmers simulate polymorphism. Then, we'll talk about a special kind of member function called a *virtual function*. Next, we'll show how this special function supports polymorphism in C++. Finally, we'll delve into advanced aspects of virtual functions. That will complete our introduction to polymorphism in C++. The next chapter examines some advanced features of polymorphism.

Polymorphism in C

We'll start by showing how you've used polymorphism in the past without realizing you were reinventing such an important concept. The next three sections show common, even mundane, techniques for using polymorphism in C.

Polymorphism with Parameterized Macros

We often use the parameterized preprocessor macro for polymorphism. Consider this one:

```
#define MAX(a, b) ((a) >= (b) ? (a) : (b))
```

It takes arguments of any type. The only requirement is that the operator >= be defined on the arguments. It doesn't matter how this operator is implemented as long as it returns the appropriate value. We can now write:

```
main() {
    int i1, i2;
    double d1, d2;
    // ...
    i1 = MAX(i1, i2);    // take maximum of two ints
    d1 = MAX(d1, d2);    // take maximum of two doubles
}
```

The MAX() macro performs correctly on these different types. This is a crude, but easy, way to implement polymorphism.

Polymorphism with Pointers

A slightly more robust form of polymorphism in C uses pointers. For example, the standard function qsort() sorts an array of any type, given the size of a single element and a function to compare elements. The complete declaration for it is:

```
void qsort(void *elems,          // array to sort
           int numElems,         // number of elements in array
           int elemWidth,        // size of a single element
           int (*compareFunc)
              (void *e1, void *e2)); // function to compare two elements
```

The parameters elems and numElems identify the array; elemWidth tells the size of a single element for swapping purposes; compareFunc is a pointer to a function that compares two array elements and returns less-than, equal-to, or greater-than zero, depending on the relationship between the two elements. Notice how qsort() makes elems a void*, to allow different types of data in the same code, and makes compareFunc a function pointer, to allow us to vary the interface to the data.

Using qsort(), we can sort any array without worrying about the actual type of the elements. Here we sort an array of strings:

```
int vstrcmp(void *e1, void *e2) {return strcmp(*(char**)e1, *(char**)e2);}
main() {
    char *names[NUM_NAMES];
    // ...
    qsort(names, NUM_NAMES, sizeof(char*), vstrcmp); // sort array of strings
}
```

The function vstrcmp() calls the standard function strcmp() to compare the two strings. We can also sort an array of ints:

```
int intcmp(void *e1, void *e2) {return *(int*)e1 - *(int*)e2;}
main() {
    int ages[NUM_AGES];
    // ...
    qsort(ages, NUM_AGES, sizeof(int), intcmp);       // sort array of ints
}
```

A simple subtraction inside intcmp() suffices to compare two ints.

Polymorphism with Type Fields and Unions

Our third example of polymorphism in C uses a single struct to represent all the different types you want to use together. Let's say you want to create a program to play concerts. For a concert you'll need all sorts of musicians: trumpeters, flautists, etc. Each musician knows how to play(), though each kind does it differently. Because we want to use different types of musicians in the same code, we represent them all with a single struct:

```
typedef struct {
    MusicianType type;
    union {
        Trumpeter tData;
        Flautist fData;
        // ...
    } u;
} Musician;
```

The Musician struct represents all our different musicians. The type field tells the actual type of musician. The union holds data specific to each kind of Musician.

We are now ready to define the interface. Here is how a Musician plays:

```
void play(Musician *m) {
    switch (m->type) {
    case TRUMPETER: printf("trumpeter plays: toot toot\n"); break;
    case FLAUTIST: printf("flautist plays: tweet tweet\n"); break;
    // ...
    }
}
```

The outside world sees one interface for all Musicians. Inside, the function behaves differently depending on the *actual* type of musician it is. We can now store arrays of Musicians, pass them to functions that make them play(), and generally treat Musicians interchangeably without worrying about their actual types. Though our code is full of generic Musicians, at any time each one is actually some particular musician.

Virtual Functions

Because C does not directly support polymorphism, the three examples in the previous section all involve some degree of hackery. In this section, we begin to see how C++ saves us from these macro machinations, casting conniptions, and type-field tricks.

The key to the last of the three solutions above is the type field which allows us to implement functions differently depending on the *run-time* type of the object. The compiler sees a single, generic Musician. We implement many different kinds, switching on the type field inside our interface functions to change the way the functions behave.

Basing the behavior of an object on its run-time type is a task that C++ takes on with *virtual functions*.[*] A virtual function is a special kind of member function. You declare it with the keyword virtual, like play() here:

```
class Musician {
public:
    void greet();        // non-virtual function
    virtual void play(); // virtual function
};

void Musician::greet() {cout << "musician says: hello\n";}
void Musician::play()  {cout << "musician plays: mmmm mmmm\n";}
```

We declare greet() to be an ordinary, non-virtual member function and play() to be a virtual function. Note that the keyword virtual is only on play()'s declaration; it is not repeated in its definition.

---

[*] Virtual functions are also called *polymorphic functions*.

Now, to show the purpose of virtual functions, we derive a class from Musician and override these functions:

```
class Trumpeter : public Musician {     // derived from Musician
public:
    void greet();     // overriding Musician's non-virtual function
    void play();      // overriding Musician's virtual function
};

void Trumpeter::greet() {cout << "trumpeter says: what's up\n";}
void Trumpeter::play()  {cout << "trumpeter plays: toot toot\n";}
```

What makes virtual functions unique is their invocation. Watch what happens as we invoke these two functions through various objects and pointers:

```
main() {
    Trumpeter t;      // a Trumpeter instance
    Musician m, *pm;  // a Musician instance and a Musician pointer

    // 1: invoking through a Musician instance
    m.greet();        // prints "musician says: hello"
    m.play();         // prints "musician plays: mmmm mmmm"

    // 2: invoking through a Trumpeter instance
    t.greet();        // prints "trumpeter says: what's up"
    t.play();         // prints "trumpeter plays: toot toot"

    // 3: invoking through a Musician pointer on a Musician instance
    pm = &m;          // points to Musician
    pm->greet();      // prints "musician says: hello"
    pm->play();       // prints "musician plays: mmmm mmmm"

    // 4: invoking through a Musician pointer on a Trumpeter instance
    pm = &t;          // points to Trumpeter
    pm->greet();      // prints "musician says: hello"
    pm->play();       // prints "trumpeter plays: toot toot"
}
```

The comments show what each invocation of a member function prints when you run this program. In group 1, m—a Musician instance—greet()s and play()s like a Musician. Similarly, in group 2, t—a Trumpeter instance—acts like a Trumpeter. In the group 3, we make pm—a Musician pointer—point to m. When we invoke the member functions, we see that the object acts like a Musician. No surprises yet.

In group 4, we point pm at t. As we discussed in Chapter 5, *Hierarchy with Composition and Derivation*, the compiler lets us point a Musician (base-class) pointer at a Trumpeter (derived-class) instance. Now, when we invoke greet(), we see the Musician greeting, but when we invoke play(), we see the Trumpeter playing.

This is the difference between non-virtual and virtual functions. A non-virtual function like greet() is invoked based on the *apparent* type of the object. In the final group above, because the object is accessed through a pointer to a Musician, it is apparently a Musician; so the Musician greeting is invoked. A virtual function like play() is invoked based on the *actual* type of the object. In the final group above, we made pm point to a Trumpeter; so the Trumpeter playing is invoked. Another way to say this is that non-virtual functions are invoked based on the *static* type of the pointer and virtual functions are invoked based on the *dynamic* type of the object pointed to.

Let's look at another example using objects created with new and delete:

```
main() {
    Musician *pm;        // a Musician pointer

    // 1: invoking through a Musician pointer on a Musician instance
    pm = new Musician;   // create a new Musician
    pm->greet();         // prints "musician says: hello"
    pm->play();          // prints "musician plays: mmmm mmmm"
    delete pm;

    // 2: invoking through a Musician pointer on a Trumpeter instance
    pm = new Trumpeter;  // create a new Trumpeter
    pm->greet();         // prints "musician says: hello"
    pm->play();          // prints "trumpeter plays: toot toot"
    delete pm;
}
```

In group 1, pm points to a Musician. This shows when we invoke greet() and play(). In group 2, pm points to a Trumpeter. Even though pm is a Musician pointer, the Trumpeter version of play() is invoked, because the object was created as a Trumpeter. But the Musician version of the non-virtual function greet() is invoked.

Polymorphism in C++

How do virtual functions help us use polymorphism in C++? What we do is create a common base class for all the types we want to use together polymorphically. The common interface of all the classes is implemented using virtual functions. In our examples above we used the Musician class as the base class holding the common interface. This time, we make both greet() and play() virtual so they will behave polymorphically:

```
class Musician {         // common base class
public:
    virtual void greet(); // virtual interface
    virtual void play();
};
```

```
void Musician::greet() {cout << "musician says: hello\n";}
void Musician::play()  {cout << "musician plays: mmmm mmmm\n";}
```

Now that we have a base class with a virtual interface, we derive the classes we want to use together polymorphically, overriding the virtual functions to behave in ways specific to each class. Here we derive a `Trumpeter` and a `Flautist` from our generic `Musician`:

```
// derive Trumpeter
class Trumpeter : public Musician {
public:
    void greet(); // redeclare interface to say we are overriding it
    void play();
};

// make interface behave correctly for a Trumpeter
void Trumpeter::greet() {cout << "trumpeter says: what's up\n";}
void Trumpeter::play()  {cout << "trumpeter plays: toot toot\n";}

// derive Flautist
class Flautist : public Musician {
public:
    void greet(); // redeclare interface to say we are overriding it
    void play();
};

// make interface behave correctly for a Flautist
void Flautist::greet() {cout << "flautist says: howdy\n";}
void Flautist::play()  {cout << "flautist plays: tweet tweet\n";}

// continue for Pianist, Drummer, etc.
```

Each class shares `Musician`'s interface—they can all `greet()` and `play()`—but each has a different implementation behind this interface. To keep the examples short, we're simply having each function print a different message.

Now we write polymorphic code using pointers to the base class. Here is a routine to warm up a `Musician`:

```
void warmup(Musician *pm) {
    cout << "introducing...\n";
    pm->greet();
    cout << "warming up...\n";
    pm->play();
}
```

This routine will work on an instance of `Musician` or any class derived from `Musician` because `greet()` and `play()` are virtual. If we pass a `Trumpeter` instance, we'll see the `Trumpeter` information. If we pass a `Flautist` instance, we'll see `Flautist` output. We can now hold an entire orchestra in a single data structure and warm it up like this:

```
main() {
    Array<Musician*> orchestra; // holds entire orchestra
    int i;

    // set up orchestra
    orchestra.setSize(NUM_MUSICIANS);
    orchestra.setElem(0, new Trumpeter);
    orchestra.setElem(1, new Flautist);
    // ...
    orchestra.setElem(NUM_MUSICIANS-1, new Pianist);

    // warm up orchestra
    cout << "warming up orchestra...\n";
    for (i = 0; i < NUM_MUSICIANS; ++i)
        warmup(orchestra.getElem(i));

    // clean up orchestra
    for (i = 0; i < NUM_MUSICIANS; ++i)
        delete orchestra.getElem(i);
}
```

We simply make orchestra an array of Musician pointers. Once we set up these
pointers with instances of real musicians—that is, instances of any type derived
from Musician—we can use the array elements interchangeably. We can warm up
the entire orchestra with a single loop. We can also delete all the musicians with a
single loop. This is the simplicity of polymorphism.

More About Virtual Functions

Now that we've covered the big picture, let's go back and discuss virtual functions
some more.

Declaring Virtual Functions

As we said, a virtual function is declared with the keyword virtual in front of it:

```
class Musician {
public:
    virtual void play();                // virtual function
    int experience();                   // non-virtual function
    virtual int practice(int how_long); // virtual function
};
```

This class has three member functions: two virtual and one nonvirtual. Because
virtual functions allow a class to behave polymorphically, a class with virtual functions is sometimes called a *polymorphic* class.

If a derived class does not override a virtual function, it inherits the base-class version. The derived class redeclares the virtual function only if it plans to override it. Here we have two classes derived from Musician:

```
class BrassMusician : public Musician {
public:
    // play() not declared, it inherits Musician's version
};

class Trumpeter : public BrassMusician {
public:
    virtual void play();        // play() redeclared, so we must override it,
};                              // "virtual" on redeclaration is optional

void Trumpeter::play() {/*...*/} // because we declared it, we must define it
```

In this example, BrassMusician does not redeclare play(); so it inherits Musician's version. Trumpeter does redeclare play(), requiring it to override this function with its own version. The keyword virtual is optional on the redeclaration. The function is virtual, even without this keyword, because it's overriding a virtual function. This redeclaration of play() has the optional virtual keyword so that someone looking at just this class can tell that play() is virtual.[*]

The derived-class function must have the same signature as the original, or it will not override the base-class function. Here we try to override setVolume() in Trumpeter, but the type of the parameter is slightly wrong (a long rather than an int):

```
class Musician  {
public:
    virtual void setVolume(int value);
};

class Trumpeter : public Musician {
public:
    void setVolume(long value);    // whoops: wanted to override Musician::set-
};                                 //         Volume() but got signature wrong

main() {
    Musician *pm = new Trumpeter;
    pm->setVolume(5);              // problem: invokes Musician::setVolume()
    delete pm;                     //          though pm points to a Trumpeter
}                                  //          instance
```

Though the Musician pointer pm points to a Trumpeter instance, the compiler still invokes the Musician version of setVolume(). This is not a compilation error; you are allowed to create a new member function in the derived class with the same

---

[*] A function that is nonvirtual in a base class can actually be redeclared to be virtual in a derived class like this as well. As we said in Chapter 5, however, you should not override most non-virtual functions in a derived class.

name but a different signature. This is usually an accident, however, so most compilers warn you about it.

Relaxed Overriding Rules

You must always match signatures to override a virtual function. You do have some freedom with the return type, however. For example, if the original function returns a pointer to some class, the overriding function can return a pointer to a derived class:

```
class B               {public: virtual B *vf();}; // returns B*
class D : public B {public: virtual D *vf();}; // valid override: returns D*
```

Invoking Virtual Functions Dynamically

We have seen that virtual functions are invoked dynamically, that is, the version of the function invoked is based on the run-time type of the object. This allows us to support polymorphism by using pointers to base classes. But pointers aren't the only way we can use virtual functions. We can also use virtual functions and references together. Recall that a base-class reference can bind to a derived-class instance:

```
void func(Musician &rm) {rm.play()}  // invokes a virtual function
main() {
    Musician m;
    Trumpeter t;
    Flautist f;

    func(m);      // will result in invocation of Musician::play()
    func(t);      // will result in invocation of Trumpeter::play()
    func(f);      // will result in invocation of Flautist::play()
}
```

The compiler lets us pass m—a Musician instance—and t and f—instances of classes derived from Musician—to a function taking a Musician reference. Inside func(), if we invoke a virtual function like play(), the actual version invoked depends on the object that is passed: when we pass m, Musician::play() is invoked; when we pass t, Trumpeter::play() is invoked; when we pass f, Flautist::play() is invoked.

Polymorphism also works if we dereference the pointer before invoking the virtual function:

```
main() {
    Musician *pm = new Trumpeter; // points to a Trumpeter instance
    (*pm).play();                 // invokes Trumpeter::play()
    delete pm;
}
```

Though we invoke `play()` through the dereferenced pointer `pm`, the correct virtual function is still invoked.[*]

Invoking Virtual Functions Statically

So both pointers and references allow us to use polymorphism. This is because the type of an object indicated by a pointer or reference can change during program execution. Alternatively, when a virtual function is invoked through an object, there is no doubt about which version of the function is invoked. Here we invoke the virtual function `play()` through objects, rather than pointers to objects:

```
main() {
    Musician m;
    Trumpeter t;

    m.play();     // invokes Musician::play()
    t.play();     // invokes Trumpeter::play()
}
```

In this example, `m.play()` invokes the `Musician` function and `t.play()` invokes the `Trumpeter` function. The types of m and t never change, so which version of `play()` gets invoked through them is known at compile-time.

The static nature of objects, as opposed to pointers and references, can bite us if we forget the ampersand on the declaration of a reference parameter. Below we want `func()`'s parameter `rm` to be a reference so it can act polymorphically. We have forgotten the ampersand, though:

```
void func(Musician rm) {rm.play();} // whoops: wanted a reference parameter
main() {
    Trumpeter t;
    func(t);                       // results in Musician::play()
}
```

Without the ampersand, `rm` is a `Musician` object, not a `Musician` reference. So invoking `play()` on it always results in the `Musician` version. The confusing part is that, even though `rm` is a value parameter (rather than a reference parameter), the compiler allows us to pass instances of classes derived from `Musician` to `func()`. Instead of binding a reference parameter to the argument as we wanted, however,

---

* If you like, you can think of dereferenced pointers as resulting in references to objects rather than objects themselves. In this light, polymorphism continuing to work is not surprising.

the compiler copy constructs func()'s value parameter using only the Musician part of whatever object we pass.

Why does the compiler not complain if we forget the ampersand and end up passing a derived-class object to a function taking a base-class object by value? Basically, the reason is that Musician's copy constructor is more helpful than we'd like it to be in this case. Remember that Musician's copy constructor looks like Musician::Musician(Musician &src). It takes a reference parameter, which you know can bind to a derived class. So when you pass an instance of a class derived from Musician to func(), the compiler invokes the Musician copy constructor and binds its reference parameter to the object you are passing. The result is that rm slices out the Musician part of whatever object you pass instead of binding to it as a reference. This is an example of the problems that secret function calls like the copy constructor can cause.

We now know that calling a virtual function through an object—rather than through a pointer or reference to an object—always results in the same version being invoked, If you are invoking a virtual function through a pointer or reference, however, and still need to ensure which version is invoked, you can qualify the function's name:

```
main() {
    Musician *pm = new Trumpeter; // really a Trumpeter
    pm->play();                   // invokes Trumpeter::play()
    pm->Musician::play();   // invokes Musician::play()
    pm->Trumpeter::play(); // error: compiler doesn't know if this will work
    delete pm;
}
```

Here we point the Musician pointer pm at a Trumpeter instance and invoke the virtual function play() three times. In the first invocation, play() is unqualified and the actual type of the object determines which version of the function runs. Because the object pointed to is a Trumpeter, this invokes Trumpeter::play(). The second invocation calls Musician::play() because the qualified name tells the compiler just which version of play() to invoke. The third invocation is an error. Trumpeter::play() must only be invoked for a Trumpeter instance or an instance of a class derived from Trumpeter. The compiler cannot guarantee that pm points to such an object, so it does not allow the invocation.

13

More About Polymorphism

The previous chapter introduced the basics of virtual functions and polymorphism in C++. In this chapter, we continue with some more advanced issues. The first section introduces a special class, called an *abstract* class, that you cannot instantiate. The next two sections discuss some decisions you will face about when to use derivation and when to make functions virtual. After that, we'll see the relationship between virtual functions and constructors and destructors. Then, you'll get a peek at how most compilers implement virtual functions. Finally, we talk about some common problems new programmers encounter with polymorphism in C++.

Abstract Classes

In C++, we must create a common base class for all the classes we want to use together polymorphically. The base class declares the shared interface for the derived classes. The Musician class serves this purpose in our examples.

Typically some of the interface functions declared in the base class cannot be defined for that class. For example, though we implemented Musician::play() for demonstration purposes previously, it really makes no sense to say how a generic Musician plays. We must declare play() in Musician so that it can be used to write polymorphic routines. We don't, however, have to define this function if we declare it like this:

```
class Musician {
public:
    virtual void greet();        // virtual func: definition expected
    virtual void play() = 0;     // pure virtual func: no definition expected
};
```

The declaration of play() with = 0 says that it is a *pure* virtual function, which tells the compiler not to expect a definition for this function. The declaration of play() is purely an interface specification for derived classes.[*]

Now that Musician contains a pure virtual function, the compiler does not let us instantiate it. Here we try to:

```
main() {
    Musician m;         // error: can't instantiate class with pure virtual func
    Musician *pm;       // ok: can use pointers to that class
    pm = new Musician;  // error: this is also an instantiation
}
```

This code makes two attempts to create a Musician object: it declares one locally and creates the other dynamically. Both attempts fail with compilation errors because Musician has a pure virtual function. You are still allowed to use pointers and references to Musicians so that you can write polymorphic code. Because you cannot instantiate a class with pure virtual functions, it is called an *abstract* class. It is also called, more descriptively, an abstract *base* class, because its only purpose is to serve as a base class for polymorphism. Classes which are not abstract are called *concrete*.

Here we show how to use our abstract Musician as a base for two other abstract classes—BrassMusician and WoodwindMusician—and two concrete classes—Trumpeter and JazzTrumpeter:

```
class Musician {                         // abstract class
public:
    virtual void play() = 0;             // pure virtual function
};

class BrassMusician : public Musician {     // abstract class
    // play() not declared here, still pure virtual
};

class WoodwindMusician : public Musician { // abstract class
    void play() = 0;     // optional reminder that play() is still pure virtual
};

class Trumpeter : public BrassMusician {    // concrete class
public:
    void play();          // no longer pure virtual, must be defined somewhere
```

---

* The syntax to declare a pure virtual function may look odd at first. What is this = 0 stuff? It is based on the idea that a function definition is like an assignment of the function body to the function name. If we wrote function definitions with an assignment operator in C++:

```
main() = {return 0;}     // not real C++
```

the syntax for a pure virtual function (which has a null body) might make more sense.

```
};

class JazzTrumpeter : public Trumpeter {    // concrete class
    // even if play() not overridden it is no longer pure virtual
};
```

Musician declares play() to be pure virtual. Any class derived from Musician that you want to instantiate must define play(). BrassMusician does not redeclare it; so it is still pure virtual. WoodwindMusician redeclares it pure virtual again as an optional reminder. Trumpeter redeclares it without the = 0 and so it is no longer pure; the compiler will require a definition for the Trumpeter's version of this function. Any class derived from Trumpeter, like JazzTrumpeter, inherits this definition or supplies its own.[*]

Synthesizing an Abstract Base Class

Sometimes you will create an abstract class to allow two classes to be used together polymorphically without deriving one from the other. This often occurs when the two classes are conceptually similar but their implementations are very different.

For example, we might want to use our simple IntArray from examples past in the same program with a SparseIntArray. This looks like an array, but can handle a large index range that has only a few elements. Because SparseIntArray needs a data structure very different from IntArray, it is not appropriate to derive one from the other. To use them together polymorphically, we thus need to create a base class:

```
class AbstractIntArray {                         // abstract class
public:
    virtual int getElem(size_t index) = 0;
    virtual void setElem(size_t index, int value) = 0;
    // ...
private:
    // no data
};
```

The class AbstractIntArray exists solely to link IntArray and SparseIntArray together for polymorphism. It contains no data and has a pure virtual interface. We can now create the concrete classes:

```
class IntArray : public AbstractIntArray {       // concrete class
public:
    int getElem(size_t index);
    void setElem(size_t index, int value);
    // ...
```

---

[*] JazzTrumpeter could actually declare play() to be pure virtual again. Designs like this require a note giving permission from your mother embedded in the comments.

```
private:
    size_t numElems;
    int *elems;
};


class SparseIntArray : public AbstractIntArray { // concrete class
public:
    int getElem(size_t index);
    void setElem(size_t index, int value);
    // ...
private:
    // maybe a binary tree or something more exotic
};
```

These two classes add the data they need and override the pure virtual interface.
We can now write code in terms of `AbstractIntArray` and use these two classes in
it. For example this function:

```
int sum(AbstractIntArray *a) {
    int s = 0, i;
    for (i = 0; i < a->getSize(); i++)
        s += a->getElem(i);
    return s;
}
```

will sum all the elements of an `IntArray` or a `SparseIntArray`.

Derivation Decisions

In Chapter 5, *Hierarchy with Composition and Derivation*, we viewed derivation
as a method for extensive code sharing, sort of an extended form of composition.
In the final example above, we used derivation only to support polymorphism. We
did not want to share anything between the two concrete classes, except an interface. We simply wanted to use them polymorphically; so we needed to create a
derivation relationship between them. These are the two extremes of derivation:
for code sharing only and for polymorphism only. Most uses of derivation in C++
fall somewhere in between.

Derivation and polymorphism are two separate concepts in OOP. It just so happens that, in C++, derivation is a necessary piece of polymorphism.[*] This close
relationship can confuse the C++ novice by obscuring the times when derivation
should be used. In this section we'll look at a few approaches to the same problem to help clarify the issue.

---

[*] Why is derivation necessary for polymorphism in C++ and not other languages? It has
mainly to do with issues of speed and type safety inherited from C. How does polymorphism work without derivation in other languages? Often these languages have looser typing rules that allow all objects to be interchangeable (not just pointers to derived and base
classes).

Say that you are writing a program that needs a queue to store integers. In addition to a normal queue, however, you need a priority queue in which the elements come out in ascending order. What kind of relationship should these two queues have? That depends on your design.

Perhaps you just want your priority queue to be a simple queue plus the addition of a sort() member function:

```
class Queue {                    // simple queue
public:
    void enter(int value);       // add to the back
    int leave();                 // remove from the front
private:
    // some data
};

PriorityQueue : public Queue { // priority queue: simple queue plus able to...
public:
    void sort();                 // sort the elements
};
```

Here we are simply building on the abilities of Queue to create PriorityQueue. We have no desire to use these two different queues polymorphically. This is an example of derivation for code sharing only.

Instead, you might decide that you want to use the queues polymorphically. But the implementations of the two will be so different that derivation from one to the other will not work. You then must create a common base class:

```
class AbstractQueue {                      // abstract class
public:
    virtual void enter(int value) = 0;
    virtual int leave() = 0;
private:
    // common data
};
```

The concrete queues derive from this AbstractQueue:

```
class Queue : public AbstractQueue {        // concrete class
public:
    void enter(int value);
    int leave();
private:
    // maybe an array or a linked list
};

class PriorityQueue : public AbstractQueue { // concrete class
public:
    void enter(int value);
    int leave();
private:
```

```
        // maybe a binary tree
    };
```

Even though the two concrete queues are not derived from each other, the common base class allows polymorphism. This is an example of derivation for polymorphism only.

Most designs, however, don't use the extreme of inheriting the entire implementation or none of it. You might decide that you want the two queues to be polymorphic, and want to minimize the differences between them. In this case you can just override enter() to keep the PriorityQueue sorted:

```
    class Queue {
    public:
        virtual void enter(int value); // virtual, but not pure
        int leave();                   // not virtual
    private:
        // some data
    };

    PriorityQueue : public Queue {
    public:
        void enter(int value);         // override Queue version
    };
```

Here enter() is virtual and leave() is not. In this case, derivation allows us to share part of the implementation and also to use the classes polymorphically. When designing your classes, keep in mind why you are using derivation. Is it for code sharing, polymorphism, or some combination of the two?

Virtual Decisions

To make a class act polymorphically, you must declare as virtual any member function that changes its behavior in derived classes. What about functions that do not change their behavior? Does Queue::leave() in the final example above, for instance, need to be virtual or not? Technically no, because we have not come up with a derived class that needs to override leave().

But we may someday come up with a class that needs to override leave(). For example, we may want to gather statistics about how long each element spent in the queue. To do this we may create a new class, TimedQueue, that marks each added item with a timestamp. Then, in leave(), it can record the time the item spent in the queue.

This new class needs to override leave(). So we'll have to go back and make it virtual in Queue. You may be wondering when you design a class if you should plan for flexibility and make some functions virtual even though they don't have to be at the moment. The only penalty for making a function virtual is a small one of time and space. For the beginner, this slight inefficiency is unimportant compared to the design issues raised by worrying if each member function should be virtual. If you think some derived class may want to someday override a function, make it virtual. The following two sections emphasize the need to make some special member functions (the destructor and the printing member function) virtual in a polymorphic class.

Polymorphic Class Needs Virtual Destructor

The destructor for a polymorphic class must be virtual. A virtual destructor allows you to delete a dynamic class through a pointer to a base class. Without a virtual destructor, the destructor for the correct dynamic object would not be invoked.

Say we had a nonvirtual destructor in our Musician hierarchy:

```
class Musician {
public:
    ~Musician();      // non-virtual destructor: not recommended
    // ...             //                   for polymorphic classes
};
Musician::~Musician() {cout << "musician being destroyed\n";}

class Trumpeter : public Musician {
public:
    ~Trumpeter();     // also non-virtual
    //
}
Trumpeter::~Trumpeter() {cout << "trumpeter being destroyed\n";}
```

In this example, both Musician and Trumpeter have nonvirtual destructors that print messages saying the object is being destroyed. These nonvirtual destructors cause problems with dynamic objects. Below we create and destroy two dynamic Trumpeter instances. The comments show which destructors are invoked with each delete:

```
main() {
    Trumpeter *pt;
    Musician *pm;

    pt = new Trumpeter; // Trumpeter pointed to by pointer-to-Trumpeter
    delete pt;          // ok: first prints "trumpeter being destroyed"
                        //       then prints "musician being destroyed"

    pm = new Trumpeter; // Trumpeter pointed to by pointer-to-Musician
    delete pm;          // problem: only prints "musician being destroyed"
}
```

Because pt is a pointer to a Trumpeter, the first delete correctly invokes the Trumpeter destructor. This executes and then chains to the Musician destructor. The second delete mistakenly invokes only the Musician destructor because the object is pointed to by pm, a pointer to a Musician and the destructor is not virtual. To correct this, we must simply declare the destructor virtual:

```
class Musician {
public:
    virtual ~Musician();  // virtual destructor
    // ...
};

class Trumpeter : public Musician {
public:
    ~Trumpeter();          // virtual because base-class destructor is virtual
    // ...
};
```

Now the same example gives us:

```
main() {
    Trumpeter *pt;
    Musician *pm;

    pt = new Trumpeter; // Trumpeter pointed to by pointer-to-Trumpeter
    delete pt;          // ok: first prints "trumpeter being destroyed"
                        //     then prints "musician being destroyed"

    pm = new Trumpeter; // Trumpeter pointed to by pointer-to-Musician
    delete pm;          // ok: first prints "trumpeter being destroyed"
                        //     then prints "musician being destroyed"
}
```

This shows that the Trumpeter destructor is correctly invoked through both pt and pm.

The implicit destructor for a class is virtual if the class is derived from a class with a virtual destructor and nonvirtual otherwise. Here the base classes have explicit destructors, and the derived classes have implicit destructors:

```
class Base1 {
public:
    ~Base1();                      // explicit destructor non-virtual
};
class Derived1 : public Base1 {}; // implicit destructor non-virtual

class Base2 {
public:
    virtual ~Base2();              // explicit destructor virtual
};
class Derived2 : public Base2 {}; // implicit destructor virtual
```

Derived1 has a nonvirtual implicit destructor because Base1's explicit destructor is non-virtual. Similarly, Derived2 has a virtual implicit destructor because Base2's explicit destructor is virtual. So if a class is to be used polymorphically, it must either be derived from a class with a virtual destructor or explicitly make its destructor virtual.

If a destructor has nothing to do, but needs to be explicitly declared to make it virtual, its body should just be empty. Do not make a destructor pure virtual; this can cause problems when destroying derived-class objects. Here are two classes, each with a virtual destructor:

```
class Foo {
public:
    virtual ~Foo() = 0;    // no: don't make virtual destructor pure
};

class Bar {
public:
    virtual ~Bar();
};
Bar::~Bar() {}             // fine: it can be empty
```

Foo has a pure virtual destructor while Bar has an empty virtual destructor. The empty destructor is simpler and will always work as you want.

Polymorphic Class Needs Virtual Printing Member Function

Recall that printing is handled by a global operator<<() function that calls a print() member function. This member function should be made virtual for polymorphic classes so an object can be printed through a pointer to its base class. Here is how we would declare print() in our Musician hierarchy (we've added some data members to make the printing interesting):

```
class Musician {
public:
    virtual void print(ostream *os); // virtual function
    // ...
private:
    int volume;
};

class Trumpeter : public Musician {
public:
    void print(ostream *os);
    // ...
private:
    int mute_level;
};
```

In this example, we declare print() to be virtual in Musician and override it in Trumpeter. The definitions for these functions aren't any different from what you saw in Chapter 9, *Better Abstraction with Other Special Member Functions*:

```
Musician::print(ostream *os) {
    *os << "Musician{" << volume << "}";
}

Trumpeter::print(ostream *os) {
    *os << "Trumpeter{";
    Musician::print(os);
    *os << ", " << mute_level << "}";
}
```

Note that in Trumpeter::print(), we explicitly invoke Musician::print() on the second line by using the qualified name. If we had tried:

```
((Musician *)this)->print()
```

we would have invoked Trumpeter::print() recursively because the function is virtual. Casting to a base-class pointer makes no difference with virtual functions, so we use the qualified function name.

As a bonus, because the print() member function is virtual, we now only need one operator<<() function for the entire hierarchy:

```
ostream &operator<<(ostream &os, Musician &m) {
    m.print(&os);
    return os;
}
```

Inside this operator<<(), m is a reference and thus the correct version of print() is invoked for any derived class, like Trumpeter here:

```
main() {
    Musician *pm = new Trumpeter; // actually points to a Trumpeter
    cout << *pm;                  // this invokes Trumpeter::print()
    delete pm;
}
```

Even with only the one printing operator defined above, this code correctly invokes Trumpeter::print() because the printing member function is virtual. So we need only one printing operator for all the classes derived from Musician.

Summary of Member Functions

Here's a summary of how a polymorphic class should declare the special member functions we discussed in Chapter 6, *Better Abstraction with Constructors and Destructors*, and Chapter 9.

Virtual Constructors and Assignment Operators

This section explains how the destructor and the printing member function should be virtual in a polymorphic class. You do not need to worry about making the default constructor, copy constructor, or assignment operator virtual, however. This box explains why. Virtual construction means being able to create a class without knowing exactly what type it is. There is no such beast as a virtual constructor in C++. At the time of construction, the class must be explicitly given. The compiler does not even let you declare a constructor with the keyword virtual. An advanced C++ programmer can, however, simulate virtual construction.

A virtual assignment operator is allowed, but is complex to create correctly. The danger is that you might assign a base class to a derived class, causing inconsistent values in the derived class' data members. Attempting virtual assignment is best left until you are more experienced in C++.

```
class Musician { // how to declare special member funcs in polymorphic class:
public:
    Musician();                          // default constructor  (not virtual)
    virtual ~Musician();                 // destructor           (virtual)
    void operator=(Musician &source);    // assignment operator  (not virtual)
    Musician(Musician &source);          // copy constructor     (not virtual)
    virtual void print(ostream *os);     // printing member func (virtual)
    // ...
};

// not a member function, but just as important (only needed for base class):
ostream &operator<<(ostream &os, Musician &m); // printing op (not member func)
```

Calling Virtual Functions from Constructors and Destructors

If a class' constructor calls one of the class' virtual functions, the version of the virtual function defined in that class is always invoked. Consider the following hierarchy made of the classes Base and Derived, each with its own constructor and version of vfunc():

```
class Base {                // base class
public:
    Base();                 // default constructor
    virtual void vfunc();   // virtual function
};
Base::Base() {vfunc();}     // default constructor invokes virtual function
```

```
void Base::vfunc() {cout << "in Base::vfunc()\n";}        // identifies itself

class Derived : public Base { // derived class
public:
    Derived();                  // default constructor
    void vfunc();               // override of virtual function
};
Derived::Derived() {vfunc();} // default constructor invokes virtual function
void Derived::vfunc() {cout << "in Derived::vfunc()\n";} // identifies itself
```

In this example the default constructor of each class invokes the virtual function
vfunc(). Each class has its own version of this function. Both versions print a message telling that they were invoked. If we instantiate Derived with this short program:

```
main() {Derived d;}
```

we see this on the standard output:

```
in Base::vfunc()
in Derived::vfunc()
```

The first line is created by the Base default constructor invoking vfunc(). Note that
it invokes the Base version, even though the object we are creating is a Derived
instance. The Base default constructor cannot invoke the Derived version of
vfunc() because the entire Derived object does not exist yet. This also holds when
invoking virtual functions from a destructor. When we are destroying the Base part
of a Derived object, each virtual function call goes to the Base version of the function. Essentially, while in the Base constructor or destructor, the object is briefly a
Base instance.

In the worst case, you could end up trying to invoke a pure virtual function thinking that you are invoking an overriding version. The compiler catches this if you
try to invoke a pure virtual function directly from a constructor or destructor. But it
might not catch an indirect invocation. Base::vfunc() could, for instance, invoke a
function that is pure virtual in Base. This would probably terminate the program.[*]

---

[*] This is the one deviation C++ makes from type-safe polymorphism. To allow different
types to mix in the same code, polymorphism requires some loosening of the type system
(e.g., allowing the assignment of a derived-class pointer to a base-class pointer without a
cast). In C++, this loosening does not allow run-time errors like invoking a member function on an object for which it is not defined. The one exception to this guarantee of compile-time type safety is the problem of invoking a pure virtual function indirectly from a
constructor or destructor. The possibility of invoking a pure virtual function like this is also
the reason that you can actually supply a definition for a pure virtual function, though few
C++ programmers do.

Under the Hood

For those of you who learn best by peeking under the hood, we present one likely implementation of virtual functions. A compiler is free to implement them differently, but this is the way most do.

All the virtual functions in a class are collected into an array called the *virtual-function table* or *vtbl*. There is one vtbl per class. Each instance of a class with any virtual functions contains an invisible pointer to its class' vtbl. This pointer is called the *vptr*. Figure 13-1 shows an example of two Musician and one Trumpeter instance with their vptrs and vtbls shown.

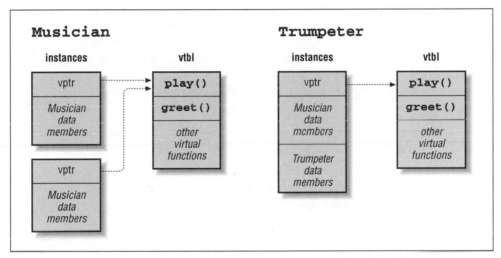

Figure 13–1: Three objects, each with its vptr shown pointing to its class' vtbl

Corresponding slots in the vtbl for Musician and Trumpeter represent corresponding virtual functions. If Trumpeter does not override a virtual function, that slot has the same pointer as the corresponding slot in Musician's vtbl. Overriding a virtual function puts a different function pointer in the corresponding slot.

A call to a virtual function is translated by the compiler to an index, through the object's vptr, into the class' vtbl. Though the compiler can resolve a nonvirtual function call to an exact function, the penalty for calling a virtual function is not that large. The biggest problem with virtual functions is that they cannot be inlined as easily as nonvirtual ones.

Note that setting up the vptr in an object is one of the tasks that the run-time system must do during object creation, in addition to allocating the object's memory and calling its constructor.

Pitfalls

Polymorphism is a complex concept. It is especially complex in C++ because of its relationship to the strong typing rules. It will take you a while to understand how to use it correctly. To help you along the way, we show three common pitfalls that novice C++ programmers encounter when using polymorphism.

Run-Time Type Information

 If virtual functions do turn out to be inadequate for a particular problem, C++ has other facilities for making decisions based on the run-time type of an object. Run-time type information (RTTI) is the name given to the collection of features that provide these extra abilities. C++ has a casting operator called dynamic_cast. (It also has three others—static_cast, const_cast, and reinterpret_cast—unrelated to RTTI but useful for other common casts.) You can use this for safe casts from one class to another. A down-cast would look like this:

```
trumpeter_ptr = (Trumpeter *)musician_ptr;          // old-style cast
trumpeter_ptr = dynamic_cast<Trumpeter>(musician_ptr) // new-style cast
```

If the cast is invalid—that is, if the object is not really of the correct derived class—this new cast returns the null pointer. The traditional cast just returns a pointer to a nonexistent object.

C++ also has a new typeid operator. This takes an object and returns an instance of a class called type_info. This object represents, at run-time, the class of the original object. It has various member functions allowing you to get information about the original object's class.

Type Fields

When we presented polymorphism in C, the most robust solution involved a type field which we switched on. Virtual functions, we said, replaced this need in C++. Often the C++ novice is tempted to use virtual functions for some purposes, but type fields for others (type *data members* to be exact, but the term is idiomatic).

For example, you might want your concert program to be able to change the volume for certain kinds of Musicians. If you store them all in a single array, how could you change the volume for just the Trumpeters? A first solution might be to add a type field to the Musician class. Then, checking this field in a simple loop allows you to change the volume on just the right instances.

For one simple case, a type field is an easy solution. Unfortunately, uses of the type field tend to multiply. If you add another kind of Musician, you'll have to edit lots of code to make it fit in. If you've avoided type fields, then just overriding virtual functions correctly is all you need to do. The new Musician will fit right into code that was created long before it existed.

As a beginner you should avoid complex problems requiring explicit knowledge of an object's type. If you cannot, first try adding a new virtual function that performs the desired work. If this would not work in the example above, then perhaps keeping lists of the different Musicians—in addition to a list of all of them—will help keep the type considerations in the creation code.

Down-Casting

For polymorphism, we are often holding derived-class instances through base-class pointers. We can call any member function declared in the base class on these objects. If we want to call a member function unique to a derived class, we need to access the object through a derived-class pointer.

For example, we stored our entire orchestra in a single array of pointers to Musicians. This is extremely convenient. But there are times when we want to use the full abilities of some Musician, say having an ElectricMusician turn up its amplifier. A generic Musician might not have a turnUpAmp() member function, even as a pure virtual. So we cannot call this function through a pointer to a Musician.

In this case, we'll need to down-cast the Musician pointer to an ElectricMusician pointer and then call turnUpAmp(). The problems with down-casting are similar to those involving type fields. Down casts make a program harder to maintain. They are not type-safe because the compiler cannot guarantee that the object is really of that derived class. Except in advanced programs, they can indicate a bad design. Their purpose might be better served with a member function. Avoid down-casts if you can.

Deriving Everything from Object

In some object-oriented languages, every class is ultimately derived from a single one, often called Object. This has a number of advantages. For example, any ability in Object is automatically shared by every class. Also, functions can easily be written that will work on every class instance.

There is no such common base class in C++. Many of the advantages of one are handled by other features in C++. Writing code that works on an instance of any type can be done within C++ using templates. Common abilities shared by every

class are part of the language itself, like sizeof and new. Creating your own common base class simply makes a hierarchy that is incompatible with any other that
is not rooted in this class.

14

Implementing an Object-Oriented Design

In this chapter we discuss how to implement an object-oriented design (OOD). OOD involves partitioning classes, and assigning responsibilities to them. We do not discuss OOD details in this book partly because it is generic to any object-oriented language, but mostly because there are entire books devoted to the subject. A technique for OOD that we recommend looking at is CRC (class, responsibility, and collaboration) cards invented by Ward Cunningham and Kent Beck.[*]

We do want to emphasize that design is a critical step in developing code, especially object-oriented code. If you try to save time by cutting corners during OOD, you will lose time during implementation, debugging, and maintenance.

Say you have completed your OOD. You have defined all your classes and their functional interfaces. Now it's just a matter of coding, right? Wrong. In C++ you have a variety of ways to implement your classes, and the differences can be subtle but critical. When should you use templates? Derivation? Composition? Virtual functions? In this chapter we discuss a technique for deciding how to make these decisions. Don't take this as the only way. There can be as many techniques as programmers; plus decisions can be swayed by far too many special circumstances for us to predict here. But if you understand the approach described here, you will be better prepared to make implementation decisions in your own project.

First, we'll give a table for making the decisions described above. Then, we'll discuss what it means. Finally, we'll give some examples that we hope emphasize the subtle differences involved.

---

[*] One place to find an explanation is Timothy Budd's book, listed in the Bibliography.

Implementation Table

You use Table 14-1 when you have defined what two classes will do, and now you need to decide how they will do it. We're presuming there is some relationship between the two classes. If there isn't, then it's just a matter of coding them. When they're related, you need to decide if you can use templates, derivation, or composition to share code between them.

Table 14–1: Choosing the Relationship Between Two Classes

If...	Then...
Two classes have exactly the same code	Use templates
You don't want all of the functional interface	Use composition
There is no change in behavior behind the functional interface	Use derivation
Otherwise	Use derivation plus virtual functions

The first question is whether the two classes can have the same code, applied to different types. If so, you can use templates. An example is a stack of integers and a stack of coatimundis. The code for push(), pop(), and any other member function of the stacks will be the same except for the type of the object they're manipulating.

The next question is whether one class (D) uses the entire functional interface of the other (B). Derivation might work if you want to add to the functional interface of D, but not if you want to subtract functions. Instead you use composition, which is making an object of type B a data member of D. Then you can define whatever functional interface you want for D. If there happen to be any pure virtual functions in B, or virtual functions for which you don't want the default behavior, then you're not finished designing. You need to define an intermediate class (I), derived from B, that has the virtual functions properly defined. Then you use composition by making an object of type I a data member of D.

The last question in the table asks whether there is any difference in the behavior of any of the functions that D derived from B. If not, then you have normal derivation. You can add functions and data to D, but there are no changes to the functional interface or the behavior of those functions defined in B.

If there are differences in the behavior, then you need virtual functions. In this case the virtual functions need to be there already in B, or you need control of B. If you're using a class from a predefined library, and the functions you want to change aren't virtual, then you can't use derivation. You must use composition.

Examples

To illustrate the use of this table, let's start with a stack class. Its functional interface consists of push(), pop(), clear(), and print():

```
class IntStack {
public:
    void push(int x);
    int pop();
    void clear();
    void print(ostream *os);

private:
    // ...
};
```

If we wanted two stack classes, one that works with integers, and the other that works with coatimundis, then we'd use templates. There is no difference in the code for any type we want to store because the stack doesn't look inside an object, so it doesn't care what type it's storing. Here is the previous IntStack as a template:

```
template<class T>
class Stack {
public:
    void push(T x);
    T pop();
    void clear();
    void print(ostream *os);

private:
    // ...
};

Stack<int> my_int_stack;
Stack<coatimundi> my_coatimundi_stack;
```

Now suppose we want an unclearable stack. It would have push(), pop(), and print(), but not clear(). The code is no longer the same for the two classes, so we go to the second question. We don't want all of the functional interface, so we use composition:

```
class UnclearableIntStack {
public:
    void push(int x);
    int pop();
    void print(ostream *os);

private:
    IntStack s;
};
void UnclearableIntStack::push(int x)        {s.push(x);}
```

```
int UnclearableIntStack::pop()              {s.pop();}
void UnclearableIntStack::print(ostream *os) {s.print(os);}
```

In the example code for `UnclearableIntStack`, we've removed the `clear()` function, and defined the rest to call the corresponding function for `IntStack`. It can be a nuisance to redefine all the functions you want. You may be tempted to derive `UnclearableIntStack` from `IntStack`, and just override the functions you don't want. Maybe like this:

```
class UnclearableIntStack : public IntStack {
public:
    void clear(); // don't do this: overriding non-virtual function
};

UnclearableIntStack::clear() {cout << "can't clear, my dear\n";}
```

We told you in Chapter 12, *Polymorphism with Virtual Functions*, how overriding a nonvirtual function doesn't always work, like when a base-class pointer points at a derived-class object. You'll get the base-class nonvirtual functions instead of the derived-class ones. So resist temptation and don't use derivation when you should use composition.

Now suppose we want a reversible-stack class. The code isn't the same as `IntStack`, so we can't use templates. We want to keep all the functional interface of `IntStack` so we don't have to resort to composition. We don't want to change any of the behavior behind `IntStack`'s functional interface, so we can use normal derivation. We just want to add another function, `reverse()`, like this:

```
class ReversibleIntStack : public IntStack {
public:
    void reverse();
};
```

Finally, suppose we want a Roman-numeral stack class. That is, it's still a stack of integers, but they print as Roman numerals. Again we want to keep all of the interface functions in `IntStack`, but we want to change the behavior behind one of them—`print()`. We need `print()` to be a virtual function. If `IntStack` was defined with `print()` virtual, or if we have control of the class and can change it to virtual, then we can derive, as in the example below:

```
class RomanNumeralStack : public IntStack {
public:
    void print(ostream *os); // override only if print() is virtual
};

void RomanNumeralStack::print(ostream *os) {/*...*/};
```

Otherwise we have to do composition as shown with `UnclearableIntStack`.

Why mess with virtual functions when composition works as well? There are two reasons. One is that you don't have to type in a bunch of lines of code like in the correct implementation of the `UnclearableIntStack` class above, making a possibly lengthy list of member functions call their counterparts in another class. The other is polymorphism. You may have a class called `IntStackManipulator` to which you can pass an `IntStack`. `IntStackManipulator` will fiddle around with the stack, push and pop to its heart's content, then it prints. If `RomanNumeralStack` is derived from `IntStack`, with `print()` a virtual function, then you can pass a `RomanNumeralStack` to `IntStackManipulator` and everything will work fine. If you use composition in `RomanNumeralStack`, then `IntStackManipulator` won't accept it.

The examples above were not very realistic or life-sized because any true-life example would contain the tiny feature we're trying to display and a huge amount of irrelevant detail to make the intended lesson incoherent. We hope you can get the point of each example in a way that makes it easy to apply to your own problems.

Is-A, Has-A

Most people like to explain the issues above in terms of *is-a* and *has-a* relations, which are two compound words invented for describing relations between classes in OOP. If class two *is-a* class one (like a trumpeter *is-a* musician), then class two can derive from class one. If class two *has-a* class one (like a trumpeter *has-a* mute), you use composition to put a class one object into class two as a data member. This way of thinking often works well, and if it helps you, then by all means use it. We find that occasionally it gets too wrapped up in linguistics and distracts from the real issue. Naturally we prefer the questions in our table, which is why we gave it to you.

Here's an example of linguistics clouding the issue: is a tricycle a bicycle? Of course not, but it might be OK to derive class `Tricycle` from class `Bicycle`. What if `Bicycle` just deals with weight and gearing? Then `Tricycle` *is-a* `Bicycle`. The sloppy part is naming the base class `Bicycle`. The name of the class should be `Thing_with_weight_and_gearing`. Then `Tricycle` would probably be called `Three_wheeled_thing_with_weight_and_gearing`. In reality we have to use less accurate names, which lose some of the essence of the class. That's why it seems more important to us to focus on the real issue when deriving.

Instead of talking about *is-a*, the real issue is whether you can inherit all the non-virtual functions in the interface without change. If so, then you can safely derive. On the other hand, you can't completely ignore the class names. You always have to take evolution into account. Somebody could come along and add something to

Bicycle that makes it unacceptable to derive Tricycle from it. Somebody can always come along and mess up your base class no matter how careful you are. You just can't feel as righteously indignant if they change Bicycle to assume two wheels after you've derived Tricycle from it. You'll look like an idiot. OOP can be hard.

Defensive Implementation

Sometimes the best implementation of a class is somebody else's. Use reliable class libraries whenever you can when you're starting out. That seems to be the way the cognoscenti are leaning these days. C++ has a lot of features, most of which are not too complicated for a serious programmer. But when the features start interacting, all hell can break loose. Your protection at the start is to use libraries of classes provided by experts. Particularly container classes, strings, arrays, and smart pointers. These will protect you from many of the dangers of C++, letting you learn it in a more benign environment. The best source of a library is usually your compiler vendor because then the library and compiler are least likely to have incompatibilities. Eventually there may be a standard C++ class library as useful as the standard C library, but it's still evolving.

15

An Example Program

It's time for an example of a full C++ program. Our example is a crossword puzzle helper. It searches a dictionary for a word with some unknown letters. The dictionary is a text file with one word per line. You specify the missing letters of the word you want using question marks, and the program tells you which words in the dictionary match. For example, if you specify ?ook, the program lists "book", "cook", "hook", etc. We chose this program because it is simple enough that the theory of the algorithm doesn't dwarf the C++ programming concepts.

The program consists primarily of five classes, plus user interface code. The classes are String, Rule, CwRule, HwRule, and Scanner. Class String is simply a wrapper around a character array. Class Rule knows how to test the crossword pattern rule that you specified, like ?ook, on a word from the dictionary. We generalized the testing by making a base class Rule, and deriving CwRule and HwRule from it. CwRule is the actual crossword rule we described above. HwRule searches for a different pattern, which we'll describe later. This structure makes it simple to add more rules for word searching. It also lets us demonstrate polymorphism. The final class, Scanner, knows how to scan the dictionary, applying whichever rule you've given it to each word from the dictionary. So Scanner scans through the dictionary, and Rule tests each word.

We discuss the classes in the next three sections. In the section after that, we describe using the program. Finally, we show the entire program.

The String Class

In this section we describe class String, the first of the classes in our example program. String is a wrapper for a character array. Most class libraries from compiler vendors include a String class, but the functional interfaces vary, so we provided our own simple version. Class String is quite similar to class IntArray, which we describe throughout the book. This should be no surprise because one is an array of integers, and the other an array of characters. The reason for the String wrapper, like IntArray, is to handle allocation and deallocation and check that indices are within the length of the array.

Here's the class declaration:

```
class String {
public:
    String();                       // default constructor
    ~String();                      // destructor
    void operator=(String &s);      // assignment operator
    String(String &s);              // copy constructor

    void set(char *s);              // set from char*
    char *s();                      // return pointer to string
    char c(int n);                  // return nth char
    int length();                   // return length of string

    void print(ostream *os);        // print string to output stream
    bool read(FILE *is);            // read string from old-style input

private:
    char *str;                      // pointer to string
    int lth;                        // length of string
};
```

You should recognize the constructor, destructor, assignment operator, and copy constructor declarations because they're always in the same form. They're the first four functions here.

Next are set() and s(). These functions are effectively input and output interfaces to the str data member. Among the reasons for the input interface is that you want to allow setting the String from a built-in string constant (e.g., "Hello, world!"), which has type char*. You need the output interface because there are library functions, like fopen(), that need a char*.

It is unfortunate that we're forced to provide the char* interface because, although we intend for clients to use the pointer that s() returns to read the data member str, there's nothing to stop them from writing. In general, you do not want to give out pointers to your private data. It's about as smart as writing your PIN on your cash-machine card, then leaving the card sitting on a cash machine. But in this case we haven't much choice—we need to interface with older code—so we do it with care.

The next three functions have analogs in IntArray. c() returns any element of the string. length() returns the length of the string. print() prints the string to a stream. We will also overload operator<<() to help us print strings.

Finally, we've added read(), which reads a whitespace-separated word from a stream. read() returns a bool, which we define with a typedef. bool is now a key-word in the standard, so eventually compilers will define it. From the parameters to print() and read() you can see we are using the *iostream* library for printing, but the *stdio* library for reading. You can find many different opinions on the rela-tive merits of the *stdio* and *iostream* libraries, and you'll soon form your own if you haven't already. We think it depends on what we're doing, and for this type of program the output seems cleaner with *iostream* and the input seems cleaner with *stdio*.

The Rule, CwRule, and HwRule Classes

In this section we describe class Rule and its derived classes, CwRule and HwRule. Class Rule defines the interface for testing a rule on a word from the dictionary:

```
class Rule {
public:
    // test word and return true if it meets the criterion
    virtual bool accepts(String word) = 0;
};
```

It specifies that a rule has a virtual function accepts() that takes a String and returns a bool. The String we use is a word from the dictionary, and the bool tells whether the word passes the rule. The = 0 makes accepts() a pure virtual func-tion in Rule. Class Rule does not define accepts(), leaving that to derived classes. So Rule is an abstract class.

Class CwRule is the rule for finding crossword puzzle words. Cw stands for cross-word. Here's its interface:

```
class CwRule : public Rule {
public:
    // member function declared in base class
    bool accepts(String word);
    // set the rule
    void set(String cmd);
private:
    // where to store the rule
    String cword;
};
```

To use `CwRule`, you call `set()` with the word pattern (e.g., `?ook`), and it stores it in private data member `cword`. Then you call `accepts()` with words from the dictionary and it returns a boolean telling whether it matches the pattern. For example, with the word pattern `?ook`, `accepts()` returns:

```
...
boogie-woogie -> false
book          -> true
bookmark      -> false
...
```

We threw in `HwRule` to show how easy it is to add different kinds of pattern-matching rules. `Hw` stands for hexword, which is our name for word puzzles made up of a honeycomb of hexagons instead of a grid of squares. Figure 15-1 shows part of one such puzzle. Letters go on the edges of the hexagons. Each hexagon contains one word. The word can start anywhere and go in either direction, but it always has six letters. Each hexagon in the middle overlaps six other hexagons, so you may already know any of the six letters for a given word. In Figure 15-1 you can see spaces for six-letter words wrapped around darkened hexagons. We've filled in two words, *dexter* and *exacts*, around darkened hexagons numbered 5 and 6. That gives us three letters—T, X, and A—of the word around 9.

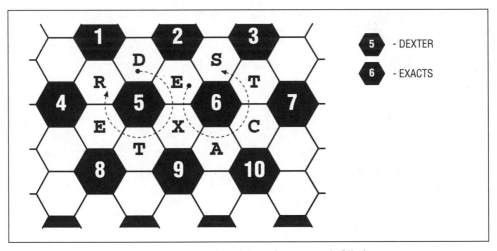

Figure 15-1: Fragment from a hexword puzzle with two words filled in

The most important aspect as far as the program is concerned is that the pattern specifies a sequence of up to six letters. Some of the letters are unknown, which we mark with question marks. We're searching for that pattern in six-letter words from the dictionary. The pattern may go in either direction, and even wrap around the end of the word. So if we specify d?x, that can match (with known letters capitalized) "DeXter" going forward, "tuXeDo" going backward, and "eXceeD" going forward and wrapping around the end. The unknown letter in the "middle" of the pattern d?x happens to match an *e* in these three examples. You can see that this searching task is similar to CwRule but is different enough to justify a new class.

The definition of HwRule looks like this:

```
class HwRule : public Rule {
public:
    // member function declared in base class
    bool accepts(String word);
    // set the rule
    void set(String cmd);
private:
    // where to store the rule
    String hword;
};
```

The interface to HwRule is the same as CwRule's, and the type of private data is the same, too. We could merge the two, but we're leaving them separate to retain independent interfaces to the rules. That way there's nothing in the way of adding a rule that has, for example, two strings in the private data, and a set() call with two strings.

Another rule you could make is an AndRule that takes two rules and returns the logical *and* of them. That is, it returns true for dictionary words that match both rules. The definition might look something like this:

```
class AndRule : public Rule {
public:
    // member function declared in base class
    bool accepts(String word);
    // set the rule
    void set(Rule *r1, Rule *r2);
private:
    // where to store the rules
    Rule *rule1;
    Rule *rule2;
};
```

*And*ing our crossword and hexword rules wouldn't make much sense, but you can add other rules for other puzzles for which logical combinations would make sense. One is checking vertical words created when you find a matching horizontal word. We leave defining this rule as an exercise for the reader.

The Scanner Class

In this section we define the final class, Scanner, of our program. Scanner knows how to scan a dictionary and apply rules to the words in the dictionary:

```
class Scanner {
public:
    // default constructor
    Scanner();
    // destructor
    ~Scanner();
    // set the dictionary file
    void dict(String name);
    // scan the dictionary for a given rule
    void scan(Rule *the_rule);
private:
    // assignment operator
    void operator=(Scanner &s);
    // copy constructor
    Scanner(Scanner &s);
    // store pointer to dictionary file stream here
    FILE *dictionary;
};
```

All our classes except String and Scanner have data members that take care of themselves in terms of constructor, destructor, assignment operator, and copy constructor. So class String has all four defined explicitly. Class Scanner also needs the first two, but we don't want clients assigning or copy constructing Scanners. So we've made the assignment operator and copy constructor of class Scanner private so no client can access them. We discussed this technique in Chapter 9, *Better Abstraction with Other Special Member Functions.*

You call dict() with the name of the dictionary file. The function opens this file and saves a pointer to it in a private data member dictionary. Then you call scan() with a rule, and it searches the dictionary for words that match the rule. This is where polymorphism is applied. scan() doesn't know which of the two rule classes you're sending it an instance of. It just uses a pointer to class Rule. The only thing scan() can do with Rule is call accepts(), because that's the only part of the interface defined in Rule. It's virtual, so it calls the version of accepts() in whichever derived class you call scan() with. That's polymorphism with virtual functions.

Using the Program

The name of the dictionary file is the first parameter to the program. How you run it depends on your operating system, but on a typical system with which you type in commands and arguments, it would look like

```
puzzle diction.ary
```

if the program name is *puzzle* and the dictionary file name is *diction.ary*. After starting the program, you interact with it by typing commands, and the program responds by displaying lists of words. The commands are two words, the first specifying the search to do and the second specifying the pattern. The search type is any word starting with "c" for the crossword search and "h" for the hexword. If the command is a word that starts with "q", the program quits. An example session follows. Suppose your dictionary has the following words in it:

```
aspect
book
brook
crook
dexter
exceed
hook
kitchennook
look
sizzle
tuxedo
```

If you enter the command c ?ook you get the following:

```
> c ?ook
book
hook
look
```

where the command you entered follows the > prompt, and the lines following it are the program's response. The c in your command asked for the crossword rule, which in this case required four-letter words ending in "ook". If you then type in h d?x you get this:

```
> h d?x
dexter
exceed
tuxedo
```

The h in your command asked for the hexword rule, which requires six-letter words from the dictionary, and in this case wanted a d and an x separated by one other letter, possibly wrapping around the end or beginning. And that's what you got.

Example Code

Here's the complete program. Following each section are cross references to the chapters that explain the important concepts used:

```
////////////////////////////////////////////////////////////////////////
// Crossword Puzzle Helper
////////////////////////////////////////////////////////////////////////
#include <stdlib.h>      // to get exit()
#include <string.h>      // to get strlen() and strcpy()
#include <stdio.h>       // to get old-style input
#include <iostream.h>    // to get new-style output
#include <new.h>         // to get set_new_handler()

// big trouble if any word in the dictionary
// exceeds this ('\0' terminator included)
#define maxwordsize 256

// These are now C++ keywords, take them out if your compiler has them.
// If not, use these definitions.
typedef int bool;
#define true 1
#define false 0

// length of hexword generalized
// You could have a puzzle with a different length, but we haven't seen any.
#define hex 6

// error exit
void oops(char *msg) {
  cerr << msg << "\n";
  exit(1);
}

// called by new if insufficient memory
void dearth_o_mem() {
  oops("out of memory");
}
```

Most of the above is just like what you'd see at the beginning of a typical C program. The exceptions are the #include of *iostream.h* and *new.h*, which are libraries developed just for C++. See Chapter 2, *C++ Without Classes*, to review the *iostream* interface, and Chapter 7, *Better Abstraction with new and delete*, to review new and delete. The printing to cerr is the only other thing above that identifies it as C++ code. See Chapter 2 to review that.

```
////////////////////////////////////////////////////////////////////////
// String: wrapper class for array of characters
////////////////////////////////////////////////////////////////////////
class String {
public:
    String();                        // default constructor
```

```
    ~String();                      // destructor
    void operator=(String &s);      // assignment operator
    String(String &s);              // copy constructor

    void set(char *s);              // set from char*
    char *s();                      // return pointer to string
    char c(int n);                  // return nth char
    int length();                   // return length of string

    void print(ostream *os);        // print string to output stream
    bool read(FILE *is);            // read string from old-style input

private:
    char *str;                      // pointer to string
    int lth;                        // length of string
};
```

See Chapter 3, *Abstraction with Member Functions*, and Chapter 4, *Encapsulation with Access Specifiers*, to review the definition of a class interface.

```
// default constructor - initialize object
String::String() {
  str = 0;                          // make nothing for set() to deallocate
  set("");                          // set() copies empty string
}

// destructor - free object memory
String::~String() {
  delete[] str;                     // deallocate string
}
```

See Chapter 6, *Better Abstraction with Constructors and Destructors*, to review constructors and destructors. See Chapter 7 to review delete.

```
// assignment operator - define meaning of operator=() for this class
void String::operator=(String &s) {
  if (this == &s) return;           // don't assign to self
  set(s.str);                       // set() makes a copy
}

// copy constructor - initialize object as copy of another object
String::String(String &s) {
  str = 0;                          // make nothing for set() to deallocate
  set(s.str);                       // set() makes a copy
}
```

See Chapter 9 to review the assignment operator and copy constructor.

```
// set value from string
void String::set(char *s) {
  delete[] str;                     // deallocate old string
  lth = strlen(s);                  // set length of new string
```

```
    str = new char[lth+1];              // alloc space for string and terminator
    strcpy(str, s);                     // copy string and terminator
}
```

We don't check the return value from new because in main() we used
set_new_handler() to make dearth_o_mem() the routine that new calls when it can't
get enough memory, and dearth_o_mem() doesn't return. See Chapter 7 to review
new and delete.

```
// return pointer to string
char *String::s() {
  return str;                          // return the pointer
}

// return nth character of string
char String::c(int n) {
  // check to make sure n is inside string
  if (n < 0 || n >= lth) oops("string index error");
  return str[n];                       // return the char
}

// return length of string
int String::length() {
  return lth;                          // return the length
}

// print string to output stream
void String::print(ostream *os) {
  *os << str;                          // op<<() already knows how to print char*
}

// overload << for String
ostream &operator<<(ostream &os, String &s) {
  s.print(&os);                        // call our print member function
  return os;                           // so you can write: cout << a << b
}
```

See Chapter 9 to review defining how to print your instances.

```
// read string from old-style input
// This routine uses fscanf() directly into a buffer, which is unsafe.
// If the input file has a word that's too long it will write outside
// the buffer. The code to do this right, typically using a getc()
// and checking the buffer size with each character, is left as an
// exercise for the reader because it contains nothing new for C++.
bool String::read(FILE *is) {
  char buf[maxwordsize];               // temp buffer
  int n = fscanf(is, "%s", buf);       // read word into buffer
  if (n != 1) return false;            // EOF or other failure
  set(buf);                            // set String to word
  return true;                         // successful return
}
```

We used C-style reading, so there's nothing new to C++ here, beyond the definition of another member function.

```
///////////////////////////////////////////////////////////////////////
// Rule: class for rules that decide if a word matches some criterion.
// This class defines the interface for the acceptance rule.
// It has no default for accepts() so all the rules that can be instantiated
// are derived from this.
///////////////////////////////////////////////////////////////////////
class Rule {
public:
    // test word and return true if it meets the criterion
    virtual bool accepts(String word) = 0;
};


///////////////////////////////////////////////////////////////////////
// CwRule: class for crossword puzzle rules
///////////////////////////////////////////////////////////////////////
class CwRule : public Rule {
public:
    // member function declared in base class
    bool accepts(String word);
    // set the rule
    void set(String cmd);
private:
    // where to store the rule
    String cword;
};
```

See Chapter 5, *Hierarchy with Composition and Derivation*, and Chapter 12, *Polymorphism with Virtual Functions*, to review derivation and virtual functions, which we use in Rule, CwRule, and HwRule.

```
// Test a word to see if it matches a crossword puzzle rule.
// The rule is stored as a String with ?'s where any character
// can match, and the rest of the characters must match exactly.
bool CwRule::accepts(String dword) {
  int i, dlth = dword.length();
  // The word must match the rule length exactly
  if (dlth != cword.length()) return false;
  // loop through each character in the rule
  for (i = 0; i < dlth; i++) {
    // get the character in the rule
    char c = cword.c(i);
    // word doesn't match if characters don't match,
    // unless rule character is a ?
    if (c != '?' && c != dword.c(i)) return false;
  }
  // word matches if all the characters match
  return true;
}

// set crossword puzzle rule
```

```
void CwRule::set(String cmd) {
  cword = cmd;   // uses assignment operator from String class
}

//////////////////////////////////////////////////////////////////////////
// HwRule: class for hexword puzzle rules
//////////////////////////////////////////////////////////////////////////
class HwRule : public Rule {
public:
    // member function declared in base class
    bool accepts(String word);
    // set the rule
    void set(String cmd);
private:
    // where to store the rule
    String hword;
};

// Test a word to see if it matches a hexword puzzle rule.
// The rule is stored as a String with ?'s where any character
// can match, and the rest of the characters must match exactly.
// Unlike the crossword puzzle word, the hexword puzzle word doesn't
// have to match the size of the rule. The word must be exactly
// 6 characters long, and the rule must match consecutive characters
// in the dictionary word, going in either direction, possibly
// wrapping around the end or beginning.
bool HwRule::accepts(String dword) {
  int d, h;

  // dictionary word length must be 6
  if (dword.length() != hex) return false;

  // For every starting point d in the dictionary word,
  // we scan forward and backward from d to see if the rule matches.
  // Instead of d going from 0 to 6 it goes from 6 to 12 so we
  // can add or subtract (to go forward or backward) then take the
  // modulo 6 to get a character position in the dictionary word.
  // If d started at 0 it would go negative and we don't trust
  // modulo of negative numbers.
  for (d = hex; d < 2 * hex; d++) {
    // at each new starting point of the dictionary word,
    // assume the forward and backward searches are successful so far
    bool fwd = true, bwd = true;
    int hlth = hword.length();
    // scan the rule, and fwd and bwd in the dictionary word
    for (h = 0; h < hlth; h++) {
      // get rule character
      char c = hword.c(h);
      // fail fwd at this d if it doesn't match exactly, unless ?
      fwd = fwd && (c == '?' || c == dword.c((d+h)%hex));
      // fail bwd at this d if it doesn't match exactly, unless ?
      bwd = bwd && (c == '?' || c == dword.c((d-h)%hex));
      // optimization - give up on this d if fwd and bwd have already failed
      if (!fwd && !bwd) break;
```

```
    }
    // optimization - match if fwd or bwd matched at any d
    if (fwd || bwd) return true;
  }
  // failed if neither fwd nor bwd matched for any d
  return false;
}

// set hexword puzzle rule
void HwRule::set(String cmd) {
  hword = cmd; // uses assignment operator from String class
}


////////////////////////////////////////////////////////////////////////
// Scanner: Class to scan the dictionary searching for words that match
// a given rule.
////////////////////////////////////////////////////////////////////////
class Scanner {
public:
    // default constructor
    Scanner();
    // destructor
    ~Scanner();
    // set the dictionary file
    void dict(String name);
    // scan the dictionary for a given rule
    void scan(Rule *the_rule);
private:
    // assignment operator
    void operator=(Scanner &s);
    // copy constructor
    Scanner(Scanner &s);
    // store pointer to dictionary file stream here
    FILE *dictionary;
};

// default constructor - initialize object
Scanner::Scanner() {
    // no dictionary to start with
    dictionary = 0;
}

Scanner::~Scanner() {
    // close dictionary if it's open
    if (dictionary != 0) fclose(dictionary);
}

// set dictionary file
void Scanner::dict(String name) {
  // open the file for old-style reading
  dictionary = fopen(name.s(), "r");
  // error if it won't open for reading
  if (dictionary == 0) oops("can't open dictionary");
}
```

```
// scan the dictionary with a rule
void Scanner::scan(Rule *the_rule) {
  String word;

  // make sure we have a dictionary
  if (dictionary == 0) oops("no dictionary to search");
  // the dictionary needs to be rewound after the first scan
  rewind(dictionary);
  // read a word from the dictionary
  while (word.read(dictionary)) {
    // check if the word matches the rule
    if (the_rule->accepts(word)) {
      // print it if it does
      cout << word << "\n";
    }
  }
}
```

Class Scanner uses only C++ features that are used earlier in the example program.

```
///////////////////////////////////////////////////////////////////////
// mainline code
///////////////////////////////////////////////////////////////////////

// The input loop. Pass it an instantiation of a scanner.
void input_loop(Scanner *the_scanner) {
    String cmd;     // command word goes here
    CwRule cr;      // crossword rule goes here
    HwRule hr;      // hexword rule goes here

    // read in typed-in commands
    while (cmd.read(stdin)) {
      // word beginning with q means quit (or quite enough)
      if (cmd.c(0) == 'q') break;
      // check for one of our rules
      switch (cmd.c(0)) {
      // c for crossword rule
      case 'c':
          // read next word into a String
          if (!cmd.read(stdin)) return;
          // set the crossword rule with it
          cr.set(cmd);
          // scan the dictionary with the crossword rule
          the_scanner->scan(&cr);
          break;
      // h for hexword rule
      case 'h':
          // read next word into a String
          if (!cmd.read(stdin)) return;
          // set the hexword rule with it
          hr.set(cmd);
          // scan the dictionary with the hexword rule
          the_scanner->scan(&hr);
          break;
```

```
        // otherwise it's an error
        default:
            cout << "unrecognized command\n";
            break;
        }
    }
}
```

The input loop could have been a class, but it wouldn't have benefited from it, so we left it as a subroutine. The only C++ here is instantiation of classes and calling member functions (see Chapter 3) and printing (see Chapter 2).

```
// The main function. Parameter argv[1] should be dictionary file name.
int main(int argc, char**argv) {
    // we want new to exit on memory exhaustion
    set_new_handler(dearth_o_mem);
    // keep things in sync while we mix the stdio and iostream libraries
    ios::sync_with_stdio();
    // the scanner we use for scanning the dictionary
    Scanner the_scanner;
    // String for dictionary name
    String dictName;
    argc--; argv++;
    if (argc != 1) oops("must specify a single dictionary");
    // set dictionary name String from command argument
    dictName.set(*argv);
    // give dictionary name to scanner
    the_scanner.dict(dictName);
    // pass scanner to input loop
    input_loop(&the_scanner);
    // exit when input loop is done
    return 0;
}
```

The main routine of the program defines a Scanner instance, passes it the name of the dictionary, then calls the input loop. The input loop reads commands, determines which kind of rule they are, sends the pattern to an instance of whichever rule it is, then calls an instance of class Scanner with that rule. See Chapter 7 to review set_new_handler(). See Chapter 2 to review ios::sync_with_stdio().

You may have to change set_new_handler() to _set_new_handler() if that's its name on your system. If ios::sync_with_stdio() is not available on your system, then delete the call to it. Earlier systems defaulted to synchronized old- and new-style I/O, saving you having to make this call, while sacrificing performance.

16

What to Study Next

Now that you've gone through our subset, you're eager to learn more of the language, right? We recommend that you get comfortable with our subset of C++ before moving on. Modify our example program if it interests you. Definitely write some programs of your own.

When you understand the features in the subset, start learning the rest of the language. We've listed C++ books and other sources of C++ information in our Bibliography. The order in which you learn features of the full language depends on your interest. The advanced-topic boxes located throughout our book may pique your curiosity. You'll find your code getting more elegant and efficient as you incorporate more of the features of C++. That's why the features are in the language.

We recommend you learn certain specific features before most of the others. This is because they are involved in some of the more important *idioms* of C++. A programming language idiom is a standard solution for a common problem. For example, here are three ways a C programmer can increment an integer by one:

```
i++;
i += 1;
i = i + 1;
```

Each solution works, but the first is the proper C idiom. The other two solutions would indicate that the programmer is still a novice to C.

The way we showed you to solve some problems in C++ are perfectly acceptable while you're learning the language. But before you graduate to industrial-strength programming you'll need to set aside the easily learned methods (like i = i + 1) and learn the proper idiom (like i++).

The following sections discuss the critical idioms you may want to learn first. We've shown them earlier in advanced-topic boxes, but we're repeating them here because we recommend you study them next. We didn't include these in our subset because we don't think they're safe enough to use when first learning C++. They look harmless, and by themselves they are, but in combination with other features they can have subtle and surprising interactions.

const

We discussed the keyword const in the "const" box in Chapter 2. const extends the type system to allow you to specify which data is read-only. When you create your own class, you can decide just which member functions are appropriate to call on const instances. So C++ allows you to extend the notion of read-only to user-defined types.

inline

We discussed the keyword inline in the "inline Functions" box in Chapter 3. inline functions allow a programmer to create functional interfaces without sacrificing speed. They replace many uses of #define with parameters.

Constructors with Parameters

We discussed constructors with parameters in the box entitled "Constructors with Parameters" in Chapter 9. While you're learning C++, we recommend defining a variable and initializing it in separate steps. But for reasons of efficiency, safety, and readability, you'll want to learn to use constructors with parameters. They allow you to define the variable and initialize it at the same time.

Member Initialization Lists

We discussed member initialization lists in the box called "Efficient Copy Constructor with Member Initialization Lists" in Chapter 9. Once you learn to use constructors with parameters, you'll want to control construction of a class' members. Member initialization lists give you control over which constructor a class' constructor chains to in each of its members.

Efficient Copy Constructor

Once you learn member initialization lists, you can make your copy constructors more efficient. Instead of using default construction followed by assignment, you'll be able to directly copy construct a class' members.

Special Member Functions

In general, the special member functions look a bit different than we taught you. The assignment operator, copy constructor, and printing operator all take a const parameter. The assignment operator returns the object it assigned to so that assignment can look like a = b = c. The printing operator is usually made a friend function of the class when the print() member function doesn't need to be virtual. We discuss friend functions in the "Friend Functions" box in Chapter 4.

So those are the first topics outside our subset that we recommend you study. If we've done our job right, you'll be able to learn these features and the rest of the C++ language more easily by building on our solid foundation. We hope it will be more fun, too. Good luck!

A

C++ Operators

Below is a list of all C++ operators in decreasing precedence. All are left associative, except the assignment and unary operators and the conditional operator (?:).

Precedence	Operator	Comment
1	`::`	Scope (Chapter 3)
2	`-> . [] ()`	
3	`++ -- ! ~ sizeof`	
	`+ - * & ()`	Unary/prefix versions
	`new delete new[] delete[]`	Dynamic objects (Chapter 7)
4	`->* .*`	Member selection (not covered)
5	`* / %`	
6	`+ -`	
7	`<< >>`	
8	`< <= > >=`	
9	`== !=`	
10	`&`	
11	`^`	
12	`|`	
13	`&&`	
14	`||`	
15	`?:`	
16	`= *= /= %=`	
	`+= -= &= ^=`	
	`|= <<= >>=`	
17	`,`	

B

One Problem with Returning by Value

This appendix discusses a problem you may come upon when returning classes by value. We said in Chapter 8, *References*, that the compiler generates a temporary when a function returns by value. This temporary holds the result of the function, allowing the caller to access it. Consider the following function that uses our Id class:

```
Id getId() {
    Id id0;
    id0.set("I'm an id, boy howdy");
    return id0;
}
```

This function default constructs id0 and then calls set() on it. When we hit the return statement, the compiler calls the copy constructor to create the temporary that holds the value of id0 outside the function. After this copy construction, id0 can be destroyed.

We also said in Chapter 8 that the compiler will not bind references to temporaries. So we cannot pass the result of getId() as a reference parameter, as we try to do here:

```
ref_func(Id &idByRef) {/*...*/}

main() {
    ref_func(getId());  // illegal: passing temporary by reference
}
```

The call to getId() generates a temporary that the reference parameter idByRef cannot bind to. Most compilers will not allow this code.

That's fine, you might be thinking, I won't write this code. I promise, can we end this appendix now? No, because you will write code similar to this. The assignment operator and the copy constructor both take references, so this code is also illegal:

```
main() {
    Id id1 = getId();   // tries to invoke copy constructor
    id1 = getId();      // tries to invoke assignment operator
}
```

This code contains an invocation of the copy constructor and the assignment operator. To both, we try to pass the result of getId(). But the reference parameters of these functions cannot bind to the temporary returned by getId(). Many compilers will flag this as an error.

If you cannot call these member functions, however, you cannot store the value returned by getId() in your own variable. How do you store the result of getId()? You can replace the value return with a parameter that the user passes and the function fills in. Our getId() then becomes:

```
void getId(Id *idToSet) {       // parameter replaces return value shown above
    idToSet->set("I'm an id, boy howdy");
}
```

The function no longer returns an Id. Instead, it takes a pointer to one which it set()s. You can then call the function like this:

```
main() { Id id1; getId(&id1); // works fine }
```

Here we pass id1 by pointer to getId() that correctly fills it in.

When you become more experienced, you'll learn that the assignment operator and copy constructor actually take const references, rather than plain references. The compiler will bind to a temporary a reference that refers to a const value. We do not cover const in this book because we think this one problem of copying temporaries does not make const worth learning at the beginning.

Bibliography

This bibliography lists some of the most popular sources of information on C++. It also contains some sources for C, object-oriented programming in general, and other topics related to C++. Because C++ has changed so much since its creation, beware of information more than a few years old.

Books

Introductory

Holub, Allen I. *C+C++: Programming with Objects in C and C++*. New York, NY: McGraw-Hill, 1992.

Lippman, Stanley B. *The C++ Primer*. Second Edition. Reading, MA: Addison-Wesley, 1991 (corrections 1992)..

Stroustrup, Bjarne. *The C++ Programming Language*. Second Edition. Reading, MA: Addison-Wesley, 1991 (corrections 1992)..

Terribile, Mark A. *Practical C++*. : McGraw-Hill, 1994.

Advanced

Coplien, James O. *Advanced C++: Programming Styles and Idioms*. Reading, MA: Addison-Wesley, 1992.

Ellis, Margaret A. and Bjarne Stroustrup. *The Annotated C++ Reference Manual*. Reading, MA: Addison-Wesley, 1990.

Lucas, Paul. *The C++ Programmer's Handbook*. Englewood Cliffs, NJ: Prentice-Hall, 1992.

Special Topics

Myers, Scott. *Effective C++: 50 Specific Ways to Improve Your Programs and Designs.* Reading, MA: Addison-Wesley, 1992.

Stroustrup, Bjarne. *The Design and Evolution of C++.* Reading, MA: Addison-Wesley, 1994.

Teale, Steve. *C++ IOStreams Handbook.* Reading, MA: Addison-Wesley, 1993.

Related Topics

Aho, Alfred V., Jeffrey Ravi Sethi, and D. Ullman. *Compilers—Principles, Techniques, and Tools.* Reading, MA: Addison-Wesley, 1986.

Booch, Grady. *Object-Oriented Analysis and Design with Applications.* Second Edition. Redwood City, CA: Benjamin/Cummings, 1994.

Budd, Timothy. *An Introduction to Object-Oriented Programming.* Reading, MA: Addison-Wesley, 1991.

Goldberg, Adele and David Robinson. *SMALLTALK-80: The Language and Its Implementation.* Reading, MA: Addison-Wesley, 1983.

Kernighan, Brian W. and Dennis M. Ritchie. *The C Programming Language.* Second Edition. Englewood Cliffs, NJ: Prentice Hall, 1988.

Magazines

C/C++ Users Journal (formerly: C Users Journal). Lawrence, KS: R&D Publications.

C++ Report. New York, NY: Sigs Publications.

Journal Of Object-Oriented Programming. New York, NY: Sigs Publications.

Newsgroups

- *comp.lang.c* (a newsgroup on C)
- *comp.lang.c*++ (A newsgroup for general information on C++)
- *comp.object* (A newsgroup on object-oriented programming in general)
- *comp.std.c*++ (A newsgroup on C++ standardization)

You may also be able to find a newsgroup devoted to your particular programming environment and compiler. Most newsgroups have a Frequently Asked Questions (FAQ) list that is posted periodically. These lists can be valuable sources of free and up-to-date information. It's also good idea to read the FAQ list before posting any questions to the newsgroup.

Index

About the Authors

Gregory Satir helps develop online publishing tools in the Portland, Oregon office of Electronic Book Technologies. He graduated with a B.S. in Computer Science from Brown University.

Doug Brown is a consultant/contractor in Beaverton, Oregon. He has been developing software for circuit simulation, synthesis, and testing since 1977. Doug coauthored *lex & yacc*, another O'Reilly & Associates Nutshell Handbook. He received an M.S. in Electrical Engineering from the University of Illinois at Urbana-Champaign in 1976.

Colophon

Our look is the result of reader comments, our own experimentation, and distribution channels. Distinctive covers complement our distinctive approach to technical topics, breathing personality and life into potentially dry subjects. UNIX and its attendant programs can be unruly beasts. Nutshell Handbooks help you tame them.

The animal featured on the cover of *C++: The Core Language* is a coatimundi, a South American mammal of the Procyonid family, a family that includes raccoons. For a time biologists believed coatimundis were two separate species, because the females live in groups, while the males live alone. The word coatimundi means "lone coati."

Coatimundis are the only Procyonids that are active and social during the day. They take a communal break at about noon each day. While the adults nap, the younger animals play games, chasing each other up and down trees, until they're tired enough to nap also.

During mating season, in early spring, males are accepted into the clan, and mate with several females. After about a month the females chase the males away, but they are welcomed back for a brief period after the young are born. The father joins in the grooming of the young, and in this way is able to recognize his offspring and avoid preying on them later. After a gestation period of 74 to 77 days the young are born in platform nests built by the mother. The female and her young rejoin the clan after about five weeks.

Female coatis form what scientists call relations of "reciprocal altruism," or, more simply, friendship. They care for each others' young, and for each other. Coatis bring their young down from their nests six to ten weeks earlier than other Procyonids. They are able to do so because they have assistance searching for food and protecting the young.

The long snout of the coatimundi ends in a flexible, mobile nose that is used to sniff food out of small places. They are omnivores, subsisting mainly on invertebrates, frogs, lizards, small rodents, eggs, and fruit. Their enemies include large cats, boa constrictors, predatory birds, and humans. Coatimundis carry their tails straight up, except when threatened.

Edie Freedman designed the cover of this book, using a 19th-century engraving from the Dover Pictorial Archive. The cover layout was produced with Quark XPress 3.3 using the ITC Garamond font. The inside layout was designed by Edie Freedman and Nancy Priest.

Text was prepared in SGML using the DocBook 2.1 DTD. The print version of this book was created by translating the SGML source into a set of gtroff macros using a filter developed at ORA by Norman Walsh. Steve Talbott designed and wrote the underlying macro set on the basis of the GNU troff -gs macros; Lenny Muellner adapted them to SGML and implemented the book design. The GNU groff text formatter version 1.09 was used to generate PostScript output. The text and heading fonts are ITC Garamond Light and Garamond Book.

The illustrations that appear in the book were created in Macromedia Freehand 5.0 by Chris Reilley. This colophon was written by Clairemarie Fisher O'Leary.

Programming

UNIX, C and MULTI-PLATFORM

Books from O'Reilly & Associates, Inc.

SUMMER 1996

C and C++

C++: The Core Language

By Gregory Satir & Doug Brown
1st Edition October 1995
228 pages, ISBN 1-56592-116-X

A first book for C programmers transitioning to C++, an object-oriented enhancement of the C programming language. Designed to get readers up to speed quickly, this book thoroughly explains the important concepts and features and gives brief overviews of the rest of the language. Covers features common to all C++ compilers, including those on UNIX, Windows NT, Windows, DOS, and Macs.

Practical C++ Programming

By Steve Oualline
1st Edition September 1995
584 pages, ISBN 1-56592-139-9

A complete introduction to the C++ language for the beginning programmer and C programmers transitioning to C++. This book emphasizes a practical, real-world approach, including how to debug, how to make your code understandable to others, and how to understand other people's code. Covers good programming style, C++ syntax (what to use and what not to use), C++ class design, debugging and optimization, and common programming mistakes.

Practical C Programming

By Steve Oualline
2nd Edition January 1993
396 pages, ISBN 1-56592-035-X

C programming is more than just getting the syntax right. Style and debugging also play a tremendous part in creating programs that run well. *Practical C Programming* teaches you not only the mechanics of programming, but also how to create programs that are easy to read, maintain, and debug. There are lots of introductory C books, but this is the Nutshell Handbook®! In this edition, programs conform to ANSI C.

Checking C Programs with lint

By Ian F. Darwin
1st Edition October 1988
84 pages, ISBN 0-937175-30-7

The *lint* program is one of the best tools for finding portability problems and certain types of coding errors in C programs. This handbook introduces you to *lint*, guides you through running it on your programs, and helps you interpret *lint's* output.

FOR INFORMATION: **800-998-9938**, 707-829-0515, **INFO@ORA.COM**, **HTTP://WWW.ORA.COM/**

Internet Programming

Exploring Java

By Pat Niemeyer & Josh Peck
1st Edition May 1996
426 pages, ISBN 1-56592-184-4

Exploring Java introduces the basics of Java, the hot new object-oriented programming language for networked applications. The ability to create animated World Wide Web pages has sparked the rush to Java. But what has also made this new language so important is that it's truly portable. The code runs on any machine that provides a Java interpreter, whether Windows 95, Windows NT, the Macintosh, or any flavor of UNIX.

With a practical, hands-on approach characteristic of O'Reilly's Nutshell Handbooks®, *Exploring Java* shows you how to write dynamic Web pages. But that's only the beginning. This book shows you how to quickly get up to speed writing Java applets (programs executed within Web browsers) and other applications, including networking programs, content and protocol handlers, and security managers. *Exploring Java* is the first book in a new Java documentation series from O'Reilly that will keep pace with the rapid Java developments. Covers Java's latest Beta release.

Java in a Nutshell

By David Flanagan
1st Edition February 1996
460 pages, ISBN 1-56592-183-6

Java in a Nutshell is a complete quick-reference guide to Java, the hot new programming language from Sun Microsystems. This comprehensive volume contains descriptions of all of the classes in the Java 1.0 API, with a definitive listing of all methods and variables. It also contains an accelerated introduction to Java for C and C++ programmers who want to learn the language fast.

Java in a Nutshell introduces the Java programming language and contains many practical examples that show programmers how to write Java applications and applets. It is also an indispensable quick reference designed to wait faithfully by the side of every Java programmer's keyboard. It puts all the information Java programmers need right at their fingertips.

Java Virtual Machine

By Troy Downing & Jon Meyer
1st Edition Fall 1996
300 pages (est.), ISBN 1-56592-194-1

The Java Virtual Machine is the software implementation of a "CPU" designed to run compiled Java code. Using the Java Virtual Machine (JVM) unleashes the true power of Java—making it possible to develop additional syntaxes for expressing the problems you want to solve and giving you the ultimate control over the performance of your application. This book is a comprehensive programming guide for the Java Virtual Machine. It'll give you a strong overview and reference of the JVM so that you can create your own implementations of the JVM or write your own compilers that create Java object code.

The book is divided into two sections: the first includes information on the semantics and structure of the JVM; the second is a reference of the JVM instructions, or "opcodes." The programming guide includes numerous examples written in Java assembly language. A Java assembler is provided with the book, so the examples can all be compiled and executed. The reference section offers a complete description of the instruction set of the VM and the class file format, including a description of the byte-code verifier.

JavaScript: The Definitive Guide, Beta Edition

By David Flanagan
1st Edition Summer 1996
500 pages (est.), ISBN 1-56592-193-3

From the bestselling author of *Java in a Nutshell* comes the definitive reference guide for JavaScript, the HTML extension that allows programs to be embedded in Web pages, making them more active than ever before. In this book, David Flanagan describes how JavaScript really works (and when it doesn't).

The first eight chapters document the core JavaScript language, and the next six describe how JavaScript works on the client-side to interact with the Web browser and with the Web page. Following this detailed explanation of JavaScript features is a complete reference section that documents every object, property, method, event handler, function, and constructor used by client-side JavaScript.

Why a beta edition? This book documents the version of JavaScript shipped with Navigator 2.0, 2.0.1, and 2.0.2, and also the much-changed version of JavaScript shipped with beta versions of Navigator 3.0. The 3.0 information is current as of the 3.0b4 release. Lists known bugs and documents commonly encountered bugs on reference pages of JavaScript objects.

ORACLE Performance Tuning

By Peter Corrigan & Mark Gurry
1st Edition September 1993
642 pages, ISBN 1-56592-048-1

The Oracle relational database management system is the most popular database system in use today. Oracle offers tremendous power and flexibility, but at some cost. Demands for fast response, particularly in online transaction processing systems, make performance a major issue. With more organizations downsizing and adopting client-server and distributed database approaches, performance tuning has become all the more vital. Whether you're a manager, a designer, a programmer, or an administrator, there's a lot you can do on your own to dramatically increase the performance of your existing Oracle system. Whether you are running RDBMS Version 6 or Version 7, you may find that this book can save you the cost of a new machine; at the very least, it will save you a lot of headaches.

"This book is one of the best books on Oracle that I have ever read.... [It] discloses many Oracle Tips that DBA's and Developers have locked in their brains and in their planners.... I recommend this book for any person who works with Oracle, from managers to developers. In fact, I have to keep [it] under lock and key, because of the popularity of it."
—Mike Gangler

ORACLE PL/SQL Programming

By Steven Feuerstein
1st Edition September 1995
916 pages, Includes diskette, ISBN 1-56592-142-9

PL/SQL is a procedural language that is being used more and more with Oracle, particularly in client-server applications This book fills a huge gap in the Oracle market by providing developers with a single, comprehensive guide to building applications with PL/SQL—and building them the right way. It's packed with strategies, code architectures, tips, techniques, and fully realized code. Includes a disk containing many examples of PL/SQL programs.

UNIX Systems Programming for SVR4

By David A. Curry
1st Edition July 1996
620 pages, ISBN 1-56592-163-1

Presents a comprehensive look at the nitty gritty details on how UNIX interacts with applications. If you're writing an application from scratch, or if you're porting an application to any System V.4 platform, you need this book. It thoroughly explains all UNIX system calls and library routines related to systems programming, working with I/O, files and directories, processing multiple input streams, file and record locking, and memory-mapped files.

Programming Python

By Mark Lutz
1st Edition Fall 1996
650 pages (est.), ISBN 1-56592-197-6

This Nutshell Handbook® describes how to use Python, an increasingly popular object-oriented scripting language. This book, full of running examples, is the only user material available on Python. It's endorsed by Python creator Guido van Rossum and complements reference materials that accompany the software. Includes a disk containing the Python interpreter software.

Pthreads Programming

By Bradford Nichols, Dick Butler & Jackie Farrell
1st Edition Fall 1996
400 pages (est.), ISBN 1-56592-115-1

The idea behind POSIX threads is to have multiple tasks running concurrently within the same program. They can share a single CPU as processes do, or take advantage of multiple CPUs when available. In either case, they provide a clean way to divide the tasks of a program while sharing data. This book features realistic examples, a look behind the scenes at the implementation and performance issues, and special topics such as DCE and real-time extensions.

Power Programming with RPC

By John Bloomer
1st Edition February 1992
522 pages, ISBN 0-937175-77-3

A distributed application is designed to access resources across a network. In a broad sense, these resources could be user input, a central database, configuration files, etc., that are distributed on various computers across the network, rather than found on a single computer. RPC, or remote procedure calling, is the ability to distribute the execution of functions on remote computers outside of the application's current address space. This allows you to break large or complex programming problems into routines that can be executed independently of one another to take advantage of multiple computers. Thus, RPC makes it possible to attack a problem using a form of parallel or multiprocessing.

Written from a programmer's perspective, this book shows what you can do with Sun RPC, the de facto standard on UNIX systems. It covers related programming topics for Sun and other UNIX systems and teaches through examples.

POSIX Programmer's Guide

By Donald Lewine
1st Edition April 1991
640 pages, ISBN 0-937175-73-0

Most UNIX systems today are POSIX compliant because the federal government requires it for its purchases. Even OSF and UI agree on support for POSIX. Given the manufacturer's documentation, however, it can be difficult to distinguish system-specific features from those features defined by POSIX.

The POSIX Programmer's Guide, intended as an explanation of the POSIX standard and as a reference for the POSIX.1 programming library, helps you write more portable programs. This guide is especially helpful if you are writing programs that must run on multiple UNIX platforms. This guide also helps you convert existing UNIX programs for POSIX compliance.

"The explanations are bolstered by diagrams, tables, sample code, and end of chapter questions...[and] the best man-style pages I've ever seen. It covers all library functions in POSIX as well as ANSI C. Each function is listed alphabetically rather than hidden under some related function. Every function is also covered completely under its own heading, eliminating the need to look up certain aspects under a related function's heading."
—Walter Zintz, *Unix World*

POSIX.4

By Bill Gallmeister
1st Edition January 1995
570 pages, ISBN 1-56592-074-0

Real-world programming (typically called real-time programming) is programming that interacts in some way with the "real world" of daily life. Real-world programmers develop the unseen software that operates most of the world that surrounds you, software typically characterized by deadlines —and harsh penalties if the deadlines aren't met. When you've just rear-ended another car, it's no consolation that a sudden flurry of input slowed down your brake processor, so it couldn't react quickly enough when you hit the pedal.

This book covers the POSIX.4 standard for portable real-time programming. The POSIX.4 standard itself is a massive document that defines system interfaces for asynchronous I/O, scheduling, communications, and other facilities. However, this book does more than explain the standard. It provides a general introduction to real-time programming and real-time issues: the problems software faces when it needs to interact with the real world and how to solve them. If you're at all interested in real-time applications—which include just about everything from telemetry to transaction processing—this book will be an essential reference.

Includes problem sets, answers, and reference manual pages for all functions and header files.

Programming with curses

By John Strang
1st Edition 1986
76 pages, ISBN 0-937175-02-1

Curses is a UNIX library of functions for controlling a terminal's display screen from a C program. It can be used to provide a screen driver for a program (such as a visual editor) or to improve a program's user interface.

This handbook will help you make use of the curses library in your C programs. We have presented ample material on curses and its implementation in UNIX so that you understand the whole, as well as its parts.

Perl

Programming Perl

By Larry Wall, Randal L. Schwartz & Tom Christiansen
2nd Edition Fall 1996
700 pages (est.), ISBN 1-56592-149-6

 *Programming Perl*, second edition, is the authoritative guide to Perl version 5, the scripting utility that has established itself as the programming tool of choice for the World Wide Web, UNIX system administration, and a vast range of other applications. Version 5 of Perl includes object-oriented programming facilities. The book is coauthored by Larry Wall, the creator of Perl.

Perl is a language for easily manipulating text, files, and processes. It provides a more concise and readable way to do many jobs that were formerly accomplished (with difficulty) by programming with C or one of the shells. Perl is likely to be available wherever you choose to work. And if it isn't, you can get it and install it easily and free of charge.

This heavily revised second edition of *Programming Perl* contains a full explanation of the features in Perl version 5.002. It covers version 5.002 Perl syntax, functions, library modules, references, debugging, and object-oriented programming. Also includes a Perl cookbook.

Learning Perl

By Randal L. Schwartz, Foreword by Larry Wall
1st Edition November 1993
274 pages, ISBN 1-56592-042-2

 *Learning Perl* is ideal for system administrators, programmers, and anyone else wanting a down-to-earth introduction to this useful language. Written by a Perl trainer, its aim is to make a competent, hands-on Perl programmer out of the reader as quickly as possible. The book takes a tutorial approach and includes hundreds of short code examples, along with some lengthy ones. The relatively inexperienced programmer will find *Learning Perl* easily accessible.

Each chapter of the book includes practical programming exercises. Solutions are presented for all exercises.

For a comprehensive and detailed guide to advanced programming with Perl, read O'Reilly's companion book, Programming Perl.

CGI Programming on the World Wide Web

By Shishir Gundavaram
1st Edition March 1996
450 pages, ISBN 1-56592-168-2

 The World Wide Web is more than a place to put up clever documents and pretty pictures. With a little study and practice, you can offer interactive queries and serve instant information from databases, worked up into colorful graphics. That is what the Common Gateway Interface (CGI) offers.

This book offers a comprehensive explanation of CGI and related techniques for people who hold on to the dream of providing their own information servers on the Web. Gundarvaram starts at the beginning, explaining the value of CGI and how it works, then moves swiftly into the subtle details of programming. For most of the examples, the book uses the most common platform (UNIX) and the most popular language (Perl) used for CGI programming today. However, it also introduces the essentials of making CGI work with other platforms and languages.

Perl 5 Desktop Reference

By Johan Vromans
1st Edition February 1996
39 pages, ISBN 1-56592-187-9

 This booklet gives you quick, well-organized access to the vast array of features in Perl, version 5. Perl is a language for easily manipulating text, files, and processes.

Having first established itself as the UNIX programming tool of choice, Perl is now becoming the World Wide Web programming tool of choice. This guide provides a complete overview of the language, from variables to input and output, from flow control to regular expressions, from functions to document formats—all packed into a convenient, carry-around booklet.

The *Perl 5 Desktop Reference* is the perfect companion to Learning Perl, a carefully paced tutorial course by Randal L. Schwartz, and *Programming Perl,* the complete, authoritative reference work coauthored by Perl developer Larry Wall, Tom Chrisitansen, and Schwartz.

Stay in touch with O'REILLY™

Visit Our Award-Winning World Wide Web Site

http://www.ora.com

VOTED

"Top 100 Sites on the Web" —*PC Magazine*
"Top 5% Websites" —*Point Communications*
"3-Star site" —*The McKinley Group*

Our Web site contains a library of comprehensive product information (including book excerpts and tables of contents), downloadable software, background articles, interviews with technology leaders, links to relevant sites, book cover art, and more. File us in your Bookmarks or Hotlist!

Join Our Two Email Mailing Lists

LIST #1   NEW PRODUCT RELEASES: To receive automatic email with brief descriptions of all new O'Reilly products as they are released, send email to: listproc@online.ora.com and put the following information in the first line of your message (NOT in the Subject: field, which is ignored):
**subscribe ora-news "Your Name"
of "Your Organization"**
(for example: **subscribe ora-news
Kris Webber of Fine Enterprises)**

List #2   O'REILLY EVENTS: If you'd also like us to send information about trade show events, special promotions, and other O'Reilly events, send email to: **listproc@online.ora.com** and put the following information in the first line of your message (NOT in the Subject: field, which is ignored): **subscribe ora-events
"Your Name" of "Your Organization"**

Visit Our Gopher Site

* Connect your Gopher to **gopher.ora.com**, or
* Point your Web browser to **gopher://gopher.ora.com/**, or
* telnet to **gopher.ora.com** (login: **gopher**)

Get Example Files from Our Books Via FTP

There are two ways to access an archive of example files from our books:

REGULAR FTP — ftp to: **ftp.ora.com**
(login: **anonymous**—use your email address as the password) or point your Web browser to:
ftp://ftp.ora.com/

FTPMAIL — Send an email message to:
ftpmail@online.ora.com (write "help" in the message body)

Contact Us Via Email

order@ora.com — To place a book or software order online. Good for North American and international customers.

subscriptions@ora.com — To place an order for any of our newsletters or periodicals.

software@ora.com — For general questions and product information about our software.
  • Check out O'Reilly Software Online at **http://software.ora.com** for software and technical support information.
  • Registered O'Reilly software users send your questions to **website-support@ora.com**

books@ora.com — General questions about any of our books.

cs@ora.com — For answers to problems regarding your order or our product.

booktech@ora.com — For book content technical questions or corrections.

proposals@ora.com — To submit new book or software proposals to our editors and product managers.

international@ora.com — For information about our international distributors or translation queries
  • For a list of our distributors outside of North America check out:
  http://www.ora.com/www/order/country.html

O'REILLY™

101 Morris Street, Sebastopol, CA 95472 USA
TEL 707-829-0515 or 800-998-9938 (6 A.M. to 5 P.M. PST)
FAX 707-829-0104

TO ORDER: **800-889-8969** (CREDIT CARD ORDERS ONLY); **order@ora.com**; http://www.ora.com
OUR PRODUCTS ARE AVAILABLE AT A BOOKSTORE OR SOFTWARE STORE NEAR YOU.

Listing of Titles from O'REILLY™

INTERNET PROGRAMMING

CGI Programming on the
World Wide Web
Designing for the Web
Exploring Java
HTML: The Definitive Guide
Web Client Programming with Perl
Learning Perl
Programming Perl, 2nd. ed.
(Fall '96 est.)
JavaScript: The Definitive Guide, Beta
Edition (Summer '96 est.)
Webmaster in a Nutshell
The World Wide Web Journal

USING THE INTERNET

Smileys
The Whole Internet User's Guide
and Catalog
The Whole Internet for Windows 95
What You Need to Know:
Using Email Effectively
What You Need to Know: Marketing
on the Internet (Summer 96)
What You Need to Know: Bandits on the
Information Superhighway

JAVA SERIES

Exploring Java
Java in a Nutshell
Java Language Reference
(Summer '96 est.)
Java Virtual Machine

WINDOWS

Inside the Windows Registry

SOFTWARE

WebSite™1.1
WebSite Professional™
WebBoard™
Poly Form™

SONGLINE GUIDES

NetLearning
Political Activism Online (Fall '96)
NetSuccess for Realtors (Summer '96)

SYSTEM ADMINISTRATION

Building Internet Firewalls
Computer Crime:
A Crimefighter's Handbook
Computer Security Basics
DNS and BIND
Essential System Administration,
2nd ed.
Getting connected:
The Internet at 56K and up
Linux Network Administrator's Guide
Managing Internet Information Services
Managing Usenet (Fall '96)
Managing NFS and NIS
Networking Personal Computers
with TCP/IP
Practical UNIX & Internet Security
PGP: Pretty Good Privacy
sendmail
System Performance Tuning
TCP/IP Network Administration
termcap & terminfo
Using & Managing UUCP (Fall '96)
Volume 8 : X Window System
Administrator's Guide

UNIX

Exploring Expect
Learning GNU Emacs, 2nd Edition
(Summer '96)
Learning the bash Shell
Learning the Korn Shell
Learning the UNIX Operating System
Learning the vi Editor
Linux in a Nutshell (Summer '96)
Making TeX Work
Multimedia on Linux (Fall '96)
Running Linux, 2nd Edition
(Summer '96)
Running Linux Companion
CD-ROM, 2nd Edition
SCO UNIX in a Nutshell
sed & awk
Unix in a Nutshell: System V Edition
UNIX Power Tools
UNIX Systems Programming
Using csh and tsch
What You Need to Know:
When You Can't Find your
System Administrator

PROGRAMMING

Applying RCS and SCCS
C++: The Core Language
Checking C Programs with lint
DCE Security Programming
Distributing Applications Across
DCE and Windows NT
Encyclopedia of Graphics File
Formats, 2nd ed.
Guide to Writing DCE Applications
lex & yacc
Managing Projects with make
ORACLE Performance Tuning
ORACLE PL/SQL Programming
Porting UNIX Software
POSIX Programmer's Guide
POSIX.4: Programming for
the Real World
Power Programming with RPC
Practical C Programming
Practical C++ Programming
Programming Python (Fall '96)
Programming with curses
Programming with GNU Software
(Summer '96 est.)
Programming with Pthreads
(Fall '96 est.)
Software Portability with imake
Understanding DCE
Understanding Japanese Information
Processing
UNIX Systems Programming for SVR4

BERKELEY 4.4 SOFTWARE DISTRIBUTION

4.4BSD System Manager's Manual
4.4BSD User's Reference Manual
4.4BSD User's Supplementary Docs.
4.4BSD Programmer's Reference Man.
4.4BSD Programmer's Supp. Docs.

X PROGRAMMING
THE X WINDOW SYSTEM

Volume 0: X Protocol Reference Manual
Volume 1: Xlib Programming Manual
Volume 2: Xlib Reference Manual
Volume. 3M: X Window System
User's Guide, Motif Ed.
Volume. 4: X Toolkit Intrinsics
Programming Manual
Volume 4M: X Toolkit Intrinsics
Programming Manual, Motif Ed.
Volume 5: X Toolkit Intrinsics
Reference Manual
Volume 6A: Motif Programming Man.
Volume 6B: Motif Reference Manual
Volume 6C: Motif Tools
Volume 8 : X Window System
Administrator's Guide
Programmer's Supplement for Release 6
X User Tools (with CD-ROM)
The X Window System in a Nutshell

HEALTH, CAREER & BUSINESS

Building a Successful Software Business
The Computer User's Survival Guide
Dictionary of Computer Terms
The Future Does Not Compute
Love Your Job!
Publishing with CD-Rom

TRAVEL

Travelers' Tales: Brazil (Summer '96 est)
Travelers' Tales: Food (Summer '96)
Travelers' Tales France
Travelers' Tales Hong Kong
Travelers' Tales India
Travelers' Tales Mexico
Travelers' Tales: San Francisco
Travelers' Tales Spain
Travelers' Tales Thailand
Travelers' Tales: A Woman's World

International Distributors

Customers outside North America can now order O'Reilly & Associates books through the following distributors. They offer our international customers faster order processing, more bookstores, increased representation at tradeshowsworldwide, and the high-quality, responsive service our customers have come to expect.

EUROPE, MIDDLE EAST AND NORTHERN AFRICA (EXCEPT GERMANY, SWITZERLAND, AND AUSTRIA)

INQUIRIES

International Thomson Publishing Europe
Berkshire House
168-173 High Holborn
London WC1V 7AA, United Kingdom
Telephone: 44-171-497-1422
Fax: 44-171-497-1426
Email: itpint@itps.co.uk

ORDERS

International Thomson Publishing Services, Ltd.
Cheriton House, North Way
Andover, Hampshire SP10 5BE,
United Kingdom
Telephone: 44-264-342-832 (UK orders)
Telephone: 44-264-342-806 (outside UK)
Fax: 44-264-364418 (UK orders)
Fax: 44-264-342761 (outside UK)
UK & Eire orders: itpuk@itps.co.uk
International orders: itpint@itps.co.uk

GERMANY, SWITZERLAND, AND AUSTRIA

International Thomson Publishing GmbH
O'Reilly International Thomson Verlag
Königswinterer Straße 418
53227 Bonn, Germany
Telephone: 49-228-97024 0
Fax: 49-228-441342
Email: anfragen@arade.ora.de

AUSTRALIA

WoodsLane Pty. Ltd.
7/5 Vuko Place, Warriewood NSW 2102
P.O. Box 935, Mona Vale NSW 2103
Australia
Telephone: 61-2-9970-5111
Fax: 61-2-9970-5002
Email: info@woodslane.com.au

NEW ZEALAND

WoodsLane New Zealand Ltd.
21 Cooks Street (P.O. Box 575)
Wanganui, New Zealand
Telephone: 64-6-347-6543
Fax: 64-6-345-4840
Email: woods@tmx.mhs.oz.au

ASIA (except Japan & India)

INQUIRIES

International Thomson Publishing Asia
60 Albert Street #15-01
Albert Complex
Singapore 189969
Telephone: 65-336-6411
Fax: 65-336-7411

ORDERS

Telephone: 65-336-6411
Fax: 65-334-1617

JAPAN

O'Reilly Japan, Inc.
Kiyoshige Building 2F
12-Banchi, Sanei-cho
Shinjuku-ku
Tokyo 160 Japan
Telephone: 8-3-3356-55227
Fax: 81-3-3356-5261
Email: kenj@ora.com

INDIA

Computer Bookshop (India) PVT. LTD.
190 Dr. D.N. Road, Fort
Bombay 400 001
India
Telephone: 91-22-207-0989
Fax: 91-22-262-3551
Email: cbsbom@giasbm01.vsnl.net.in

THE AMERICAS

O'Reilly & Associates, Inc.
101 Morris Street
Sebastopol, CA 95472 U.S.A.
Telephone: 707-829-0515
Telephone: 800-998-9938 (U.S. & Canada)
Fax: 707-829-0104
Email: order@ora.com

SOUTHERN AFRICA

International Thomson Publishing Southern Africa
Building 18, Constantia Park
240 Old Pretoria Road
P.O. Box 2459
Halfway House, 1685 South Africa
Telephone: 27-11-805-4819
Fax: 27-11-805-3648

TO ORDER: **800-889-8969** (CREDIT CARD ORDERS ONLY); **order@ora.com**; http://www.ora.com
OUR PRODUCTS ARE AVAILABLE AT A BOOKSTORE OR SOFTWARE STORE NEAR YOU.

O'Reilly & Associates, Inc.
101 Morris Street
Sebastopol, CA 95472-9902
1-800-998-9938

Visit us online at:
http://www.ora.com/
orders@ora.com

O'REILLY WOULD LIKE TO HEAR FROM YOU

Which book did this card come from?

_____

Where did you buy this book?
- ❏ Bookstore
- ❏ Direct from O'Reilly
- ❏ Bundled with hardware/software
- ❏ Other _____
- ❏ Computer Store
- ❏ Class/seminar

What operating system do you use?
- ❏ UNIX
- ❏ Windows NT
- ❏ Other _____
- ❏ Macintosh
- ❏ PC(Windows/DOS)

What is your job description?
- ❏ System Administrator
- ❏ Network Administrator
- ❏ Web Developer
- ❏ Other _____
- ❏ Programmer
- ❏ Educator/Teacher

❏ Please send me O'Reilly's catalog, containing a complete listing of O'Reilly books and software.

Name _____ Company/Organization _____

Address _____

City _____ State _____ Zip/Postal Code _____ Country _____

Telephone _____ Internet or other email address (specify network)

Nineteenth century wood engraving
of a bear from the O'Reilly &
Associates Nutshell Handbook®
Using & Managing UUCP.

POST CARD

BUSINESS REPLY MAIL
FIRST CLASS MAIL   PERMIT NO. 80   SEBASTOPOL, CA

Postage will be paid by addressee

O'Reilly & Associates, Inc.
101 Morris Street
Sebastopol, CA 95472-9902

||.|....|.|..|.|..|.||....|.|.|.||.|..|.|..|.||....|.|..||.|